MUSIC MANIA

by

Stephanie K. Burton

Over 500 Easy Activities for Integrating the Curriculum
Through Favorite Children's Songs

♩ **LARGE GROUP**

♩ **SCIENCE**

♩ **MATH**

♩ **ART**

♩ **WHOLE LANGUAGE / READING**

♩ **MULTI-CULTURAL**

♩ **LITERATURE**

PLUS 26 REPRODUCIBLE MINI-BOOKS

Acknowledgements

Thanks to:

My husband Andrew, and children Lindsey and Joshua for putting up with my spending so many hours in front of the computer;

My parents Lois and Norman Kay for their continuing support of my project;

Phyllis Campbell for proofreading and additional suggestions;

Jane Neff for answering computer questions;

The many children I've taught whose enthusiasm for music and learning never ends;

Teachers who used my first book **MUSIC EXPLOSION** and encouraged me to write another book.

© 1994 Stephanie Burton

Music Mania Book ISBN 1-889163-02-3

Music Mania Book and Tape Set ISBN 1-889163-00-7

To Andrew, Lindsey, and Joshua

> **Sing a song together,**
> **Just you and I will sing,**
> **For when we sing together,**
> **We can do most anything.**
>
> Stephanie Burton

About the Author

Stephanie K. Burton grew up near Cleveland, Ohio, but has lived in Colorado since attending Colorado College where she received a B.A. and and M.A.T. She and her family live in Manitou Springs, a beautiful town at the base of Pike's Peak. Stephanie currently teaches preschool in a public school in Colorado Springs, in addition to presenting workshops and inservices at conferences and schools around the country.

Her first book, MUSIC EXPLOSION (1994. Perfection Learning Corp.) received the 1994 Early Childhood News Director's Award. Her third book, SCIENCE TIMES WITH NURSERY RHYMES, co-authored with Phyllis Campbell is fast becoming a favorite with early childhood teachers.

For information on publications, workshops or children's mini-conferences contact:

Panda Bear Publications
P.O. Box 391
Manitou Springs, CO 80829
(719) 685-3319
FAX: (719) 685-4427
E-MAIL: burtfam@ix.netcom.com

CONTENTS

What do children say when they've just been truly motivated and have had a wonderful learning experience? "LET'S DO IT AGAIN!" Those words are music to a teacher's ears because teachers know that the best learning takes place when children are interested in and tuned in to what they're learning. **MUSIC MANIA** is full of fun songs and fantastic activities that will leave your students saying, "Let's Do It Again."

Music is a magical motivational tool for children. It stimulates their mind and body with melody, tempo, pitch, and beat, and in doing so, integrates all the learning modes. **MUSIC MANIA** gets the children excited and motivated to learn more. By using music as the introductory motivator, further exploration into subject areas becomes a natural extension of the songs. The use of traditional songs enables the students to begin the exploration in an area with which they are already familiar and comfortable, while the introduction of new songs can be challenging, fun and rewarding.

In my first book **MUSIC EXPLOSION** (1994, Perfection Learning Corp.) I chose what I felt to be the "all time greatest hits" of traditional children's songs. Teachers who have used the book have found it to be extremely helpful and fun to use in the classroom. In fact, at the 1992 Colorado Kindergarten Teacher's Conference several of them made me promise to have a second book ready for their 1993 Conference. As a result of peer pressure,(so much for teaching children to stand up to their contemporaries, a true case of "Do as I say, not as I do!) my second book, **MUSIC MANIA** was born. **MUSIC MANIA** includes more timeless traditional tunes plus a few new songs that have been favorites in my own classroom. As in my first book, the activities in **MUSIC MANIA** adhere to the guidelines for developmentally appropriate practices set by the NAEYC. The songs and activities have even been field tested in my own classroom which consists of a combination of special education, at-risk, and gifted 3-5 year olds.

The wonderful thing about music is that each child can enjoy it and expand on it as far as their own developmental level will allow. If it seems too difficult, simplify it; if it seems too easy, let the children go a step further with the music by adding instruments, movements, and writing new verses. When using the music as a starting point for other curriculum areas, get the children to think about the words carefully. What do the words mean? Are there any new words or concepts to discuss? What different things are talked about in the song that you might want to study further?

MUSIC MANIA consists of 26 children's songs, most of which will already be familiar to you and to the children in your class. Each song is followed by suggestions for activities to extend the song into various curriculum areas. The activities follow guidelines set by NAEYC in their publication **Developmental-ly Appropriate Practices in Early Childhood Programs Serving Children Birth Through Age 8.**

At the end of the book you will find reproducible mini-books containing the words to each song and an open-ended activity to complete. I strongly encourage you to have the children take the mini-books home to share with their parents. You will find that most of the parents in your class know these songs and will love to see the words so that they may sing along with their child. In addition to the benefit of including parents in the child's school education, you are providing the young beginning reader with the word association for songs they have already memorized.

The songs are first presented in the traditional form in a voice range that should be comfortable for most children. I have also included chords for autoharp or guitar and chord diagrams for the guitar. The guitar chords are easy enough for any beginning guitarist.

Each song unit is divided into several curriculum areas as outlined below:

> *LARGE GROUP TIME* - These are ways to extend the song beyond the traditional presentation. It includes ideas for adding movement, changing words, using instruments, and personalizing the song. Many of the activities were suggested by the children in my class. Watch and listen to the children as you are singing in a large group. Try out their ideas and suggestions and you'll find yourself with a whole new repertoire.

> *CURRICULUM INTEGRATION-* Teachers using a theme-based curriculum will find this useful as a guide to what theme units can be used with each song.

> *SCIENCE-* Children learn best by a hands-on approach to learning. The science activities involve exploration and discovery. Many of them depend on following the scientific process of prediction, observation and hypothesis. Although your students may not yet be able to write down their own words, they can dictate to an adult or make drawings to illustrate their predictions and observations.

MATH- As with science, children need to explore and experience a hands-on approach to math if they are to gain a true understanding of math concepts. The children must understand the concrete basics of mathematics by using manipulatives before they can be expected to perform abstract mathematical functions with pencil and paper. The activities in this section involve counting, sorting, classifying, matching, distinguishing same and different, more and less, and simple addition and subtraction. The ability of the child(ren) with whom you are working should determine the complexity or simplicity of any of these activities. Any of the activities can be simplified or made more challenging as needed for a particular group.

ART- All of the art activities are process oriented rather than product oriented. Have you ever marveled at the child who spends a half hour to work on a painting only to leave it crumpled up at school for weeks? Young children are much more interested in the process of the artwork and until they reach a certain developmental level, the final outcome or product is irrelevant. It is for this reason that "arts and crafts" projects where very young children must copy a model set before them should be used only on rare occasions, if at all. You will know if you are on the right track if the children are having fun with the art materials and feel free to express themselves creatively. If the children or the teacher seem to be getting frustrated by the art experience, you need to take a step back and see if there was too much emphasis on the final product.

WHOLE LANGUAGE / READING- This section includes ways to encourage children to correlate the spoken word to the written word in a natural, non-threatening environment. I often refer to making word charts while brainstorming with the children. Even if your children don't recognize letters yet, it helps them to see their ideas presented in the written form. I usually try to draw little pictures next to the words so that the children can "read" the word chart back to me. (I'm a lousy artist and the children love to laugh at my drawings.)

Making books with children is an effective and fun way to encourage reading for readers and non-readers alike. Children who are not yet writing words can dictate the text to an adult or older student who will write down the child's exact words. Children who are able to write their own text can do so. Illustrations can be added using the child's drawings, paintings, or cut out magazine pictures, or an older student or adult can illustrate the child's text. Class books are books in which each child contributes a page. Individual books are books that each child creates for him/herself.

MULTI-CULTURAL- Wherever possible, I have added activities to help acquaint children with cultures other than their own. Some of the activities involve exploring life in other countries, some involve looking at the different cultures in our own country, and some consist of learning words in a foreign language. I encourage you to ask the parents in the class to share their own knowledge and experience with the class in order to enrich the children's awareness of and sensitivity to other cultures.

RELATED ACTIVITIES- This includes activities such as field trips, guest speakers, family involvement activities and interest centers that may help to enrich the song unit.

RELATED MUSIC- These are additional songs that can add another dimension to your song unit. The music under this heading follows similar themes or concepts to those in the original song.

RELATED LITERATURE- Here is just a sample of books related to themes in the song that you might want to read to your class. Storytime should be a scheduled part of every class session, not an add on "if there is time." There are so many wonderful children's books available and more being published every month that I encourage you to ask your librarian for additional suggestions. There is a new trend in children's books to publish storybooks based on children's songs. If you are fortunate enough to find these, sing the books to the children instead of reading them. The children will be enthralled.

(SINGING WITH YOUNG CHILDREN)

Anyone can learn to enjoy singing with children-- yes, that includes you! One great thing about singing with young children is that most of them love to sing, so you're already one step ahead . The other wonderful part of singing with young children is that they don't care what you're voice sounds like! You can sing in tune or out of tune and as long as the children see that you're enjoying the songs, they'll join right in.

For those people who feel it's just too intimidating to sing in front of a group, use a puppet. Make the puppet sing instead of you. That way you're not putting yourself on the line. Puppets can have any kind of voice: gruff, rough, sweet, silly, low or high. Another useful tool for those feeling hesitant, is to accompany yourself with an instrument. An instrument serves as a focus for the children and gives you something to hold onto. You can use a rhythm instrument, such as rhythm sticks, a tambourine or hand drum. An autoharp is very easy to play. It has a lovely sound and all you have to do is press some buttons and strum. You might want to try playing guitar. In order to play most children's songs on guitar, you just need to know five or six beginning chords. Don't forget, you're not auditioning for Carnegie Hall. Your audience will be very accepting and they already think you're great.

When teaching songs to children follow these simple steps:
1. Sing the song yourself.
2. Sing the song line by line and have the children echo you.
3. Sing the song again, this time with the children.
4. Expand on the traditional song by adding motions, writing new words, using props, dramatizing, varying the tempo or pitch.

You may want to work on a song for more than one day before reaching step four. Children love repetition, so although you may be getting tired of doing the same song, if the children are still enjoying it, just keep going. Believe it or not, in my classroom the children insist we sing "What Are You Wearing" by Hap Palmer and my own composition "I'm Me, I'm Special" every day. When I get tired of it, I go to step four and adapt the song so that I can remain interested in it.

The most important thing of all is--have fun!! No matter what you're teaching, if the children see that you're enthusiastic, they will be too.

Happy Singing,

Stephanie Burton

APPLES AND BANANAS

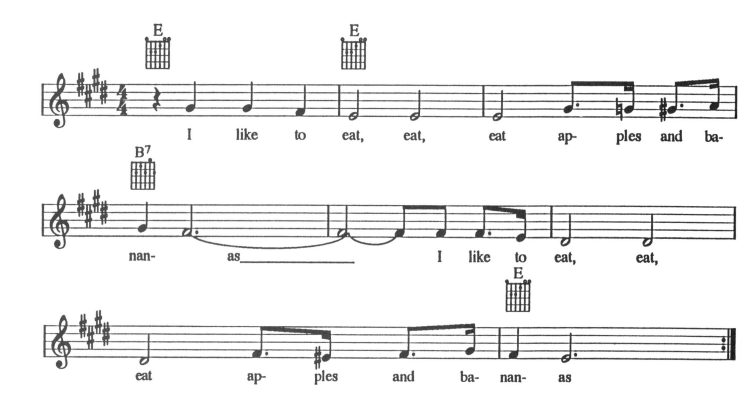

2. I like to ate...aypuls and banaynays.
3. I like to eet...eeples and baneenees.
4. I like to ite...iples and baninis.

6. I like to ote...oples and banonos.
7. I like to ute...uples and banunus.

(LARGE GROUP TIME)

MAKE UP MOTIONS. Ask the children to make up motions or make their bodies into the shape of an apple or banana for the words *apples* and *bananas.*

SING IN TWO GROUPS. One group sings the word *apples* and the other group answers with the word *bananas.*

SIGN LANGUAGE. Learn the sign language for this song and learn signs for other foods about which the children might want to sing. A special education teacher or your local Center on Deafness might be able to help you out.

USE A CHILD'S NAME. Instead of singing "I like to eat," ask a child what he/she likes to eat and sing about it: Anne likes to eat, eat, eat pizza and spaghetti...

SING ABOUT THE FIVE SENSES. Use this song when learning about the five senses. Ask children to tell what to sing about for each of the senses. " I like to see, see, see (or taste, smell, touch, hear.)"

CURRICULUM INTEGRATION

NUTRITION
APPLES
FIVE SENSES

SCIENCE

SEED COLLECTION. Send home a note asking parents to send in a variety of seeds from various fruits and vegetables. See if the children can identify from which food each type of seed came.

APPLE DISPLAY AND TASTING. There are many, many different varieties of apples including: red delicious, yellow delicious, rome, pippin, Granny Smith, Jonathan, etc. Collect as many of these as you can and make a display on your science table. Have the children taste a piece of each variety.

APPLESAUCE. Peel and cut 1/2 apple per child. Boil or steam apples until very soft. Mash apples with ricer, food processor or blender. If too tart, add a touch of honey or sugar.

MATH

GRAPH. Ask the children to indicate on a graph which fruit they like the best, apples or bananas. You can make apple or banana cut outs for them to place on a square in the graph. Which was liked by the most children? Which was liked by the fewest children?

SEED PATTERNS. Using actual seeds or cut out pictures of seeds make a pattern. Have the children predict which seed will come next:
          apple, orange, apple, orange, _____
For older children, make the pattern more complicated. The children can also take a variety of seeds and make up their own patterns.

SORT AND CLASSIFY. The children can sort and classify a variety of seeds. You can either buy them in seed packets or have parents send them in. Each child can bring in an apple from home to sort, count and classify.

(ART)

APPLE PRINTS. Cut apples in halves and in wedges. Children dip them into paint and press onto paper for and apple design.

APPLE SEED COLLAGE. Cut red, yellow or green construction paper into the shape of an apple. Collect apple seeds from families or buy some from a plant nursery or craft store. Children can glue the seeds on the paper for an apple seed collage.

APPLE AND BANANA CUT OUTS. Give the children magazines and let them look for and cut out pictures of apples and bananas. They can glue them onto paper plates. Younger children can just look for pictures of any kind of fruit.

(WHOLE LANGUAGE / READING)

COMPARING APPLES TO BANANAS. Look at the outside and inside of an apple and an orange. On the board or a word chart, label one side *apple* and the other side *banana*. As the children make observations about each fruit, write their words in the appropriate column. You can also have one section read *same* and other read *different*. How are apples and bananas alike? How are they different?

CHANGING VOWEL SOUNDS. Change the vowel sounds in common words so that the children hear how it can change the meaning of the word:
> doll- dayl, deel, dile, dole, dule
> baby- babay, beebee, bibi, bobo, bubu

Take the childrens' names and change the vowels. A fun song with which to do this is "Willaby Wallaby Woo" and "The Name Game."

FIVE SENSES BOOK. Using the verses you may have written at large group time, create a book by writing the words and having the children illustrate:
> I like eat... apples and bananas.
> I like to smell... roses and pizza
> I like to touch... puppies and kittens
> I like to see...smiles and rainbows
> I like to hear...music and laughter

MULTI-CULTURAL

INTERNATIONAL TREATS. Try foods made with apples or bananas that come from other cultures. Ask parents and grandparents to share their ethnic apple and banana specialties with the class. For instance, in France they eat apple tarts and bananas flambe. In Puerto Rico, fried plantain, which is a type of banana, is a staple. In Germany, apple pancakes are a favorite.

RELATED ACTIVITIES

SNACKTIME. Prepare apples and bananas in a variety of ways. Bananas can be raw, mashed, fried with a cinnamon sugar coating, or made into banana bread. Apples can be raw, baked with cinnamon and sugar, made into applesauce, baked in banana bread. Have the children make and serve a fruit salad made only of apples and bananas.

RELATED MUSIC

The Name Game (Banana Fanna Song)
Willaby Wallaby Woo
Tummy Tango (by Greg and Steve)
Way Up High in the Apple Tree

RELATED LITERATURE

Aliki. (1963). **THE STORY OF JOHNNY APPLESEED.** Canada: Prentice.

Carle, Eric. (1986). **THE VERY HUNGRY CATERPILLAR.** N.Y.: Philomel.

Carle, Eric. (1985). **THE GREEDY PYTHON.** N.Y.: Scholastic.

Ehrlert, Lois. (1989). **EATING THE ALPHABET.** San Diego: Harcourt.

Gibbons, Gail. (1984). **THE SEASONS OF ARNOLD'S APPLE TREE.** San Diego: Harcourt, Brace, Jovanovich.

BABY BIRD

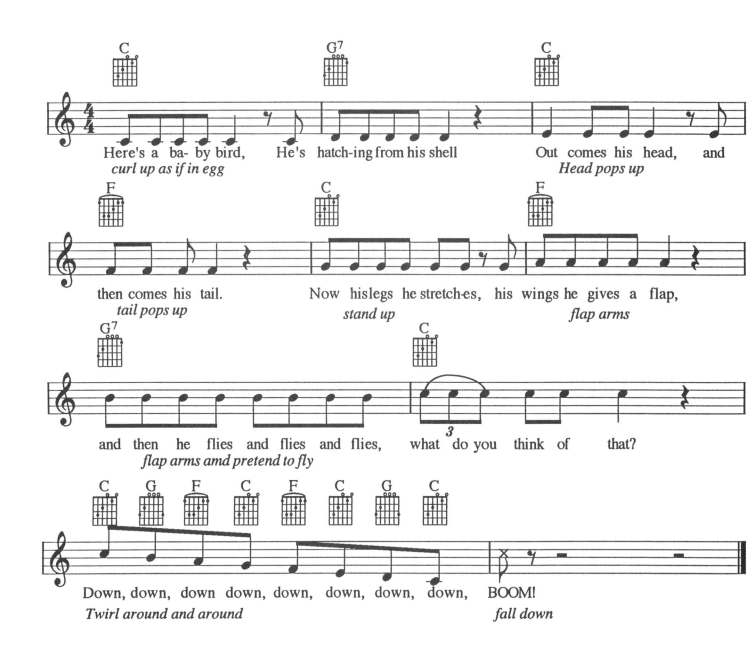

Here's a ba-by bird, He's hatch-ing from his shell
curl up as if in egg

Out comes his head, and
Head pops up

then comes his tail.
tail pops up

Now his legs he stretch-es, his wings he gives a flap,
stand up *flap arms*

and then he flies and flies and flies, what do you think of that?
flap arms amd pretend to fly

Down, down, down down, down, down, down, down, BOOM!
Twirl around and around *fall down*

(**LARGE GROUP TIME**)

FAST AND SLOW. Sing the song at various tempos: slow, medium and fast. Have the children move according to the tempo.

HERE'S A BABY CHICK. If possible, incubate some chicken eggs and watch them hatch or visit a feed store where they hatch eggs. Change the words to "Here's a baby chick."

WHAT ELSE HATCHES FROM EGGS? Ask the children what else hatches from eggs. Change the words accordingly. Here's an example:

> Here's a baby snake. It's hatching from its shell.
> Out pops its head, then comes its tail.
> Now he wiggles, wiggles,
> He's getting very long.
> Now he slithers, slithers
> All along the ground,
> s-s-s-s-s-s-s-s-s-s-s
>
> Here's a baby dinosaur. Its hatching from its shell,
> Out pops her head and then comes her tail.
> Then she walks and walks and walks, she really shakes the ground,
> I wonder where she's going now, she's looking all around.
> Stomp, stomp, stomp... roar!

CURRICULUM INTEGRATION

EGGS
BABY ANIMALS
SPRING
DINOSAURS (change the words)

SCIENCE

HATCH SOME EGGS. Purchase, borrow or rent an incubator in which to hatch some eggs. Have the children predict how many eggs will hatch. (It is unusual for all of the eggs to hatch.) After, the eggs have hatched, see who was correct.

EGGS, EGGS, AND MORE EGGS. Examine raw and cooked eggs: scrambles, hard boiled, fried, etc. What is similar? What is different?

SPINNING EGGS. Demonstrate and let the children experiment with the way a raw egg spins on a table versus how a hard boiled egg spins. Why do they think they spin differently?

EGG SOUND SHAKERS. Fill plastic eggs with different objects such as, paper clips, rubber bands, marbles. Make two eggs filled with each item. The children shake them and see if they can pick out the two eggs whose sounds match.

RUBBER EGGS. Place a raw egg in a jar of vinegar. Leave for 24 hours. Remove carefully, touch gently. Watch it bounce.

MATH

FILLING EGGS. Write a numeral on each plastic egg. Provide the children with beans, marbles, paper clips, something small to fit in an egg. The children count out the appropriate number of items for each egg. For three year olds and young four year olds, tape colors, shapes or animal pictures on a shell and the children will place the matching item inside the egg.

EGG MATCHING. Cut out matching pairs of egg shapes from wallpaper, fabric or construction paper. The children will enjoy finding the matching pairs.

SERIATE EGGS. Cut out egg shapes of varying heights or widths and have the children put them in order according to size. ○ ○ ○

CHEAPER BY THE DOZEN. Talk about how people usually buy eggs by the dozen. How many are in a dozen? Bring in a dozen eggs and count them together. Ask the children to bring in a dozen of one item.

EGG CARTON COUNTING. Using egg cartons, encourage the children to place and count small items i.e. bear counters, beans or small blocks, in each compartment.

EGG PUZZLES. Cut egg shapes out of various sizes, colors, or patterns of paper. Decorate them with crayons, markers or watercolors. Cut them in half, thirds or fourths using zigzag patterns to make puzzles.

ART

DECORATE EGG CUTOUTS. Provide the children with egg shapes drawn on paper for them to cut out. They can decorate them with paints, markers, crayons, or collage materials.

EGG DYING. Children love to dye hard-boiled eggs even if it isn't Easter. Place eggs in food coloring to which you have added one tablespoon of vinegar.

EGG SHELL COLLAGE. Ask parents to send in washed and dried egg shells. Crumble the shells and color with food coloring. The children can glue the colored bits of shell on paper or foam trays.

WHOLE LANGUAGE / READING

WORD CHART. Brainstorm with the children all the animals that hatch from eggs. Write their ideas on chart paper or the chalkboard.

ALL ABOUT EGGS. The children can create individual or class books about eggs. Their books could be about different sizes, shapes, and colors of eggs, or about the different animals that hatch from eggs. They can dictate the text, or if your students are older, they can write the text themselves. You can use egg shaped paper for the pages.

HUMPTY DUMPTY. Recite and act out the words to HUMPTY DUMPTY. Write the words with accompanying pictures on chart paper or on word cards in a pocket chart, so that children can see the correlation of the spoken word to the written word.

MULTI-CULTURAL

EGGS AROUND THE WORLD. Many different countries and cultures pride themselves on their handcrafted eggs. Russian eggs are wooden, painted, and lacquered; from Far Eastern countries you can get onyx eggs; the French are famous for their delicate Faberge eggs. Ask parents to send in any decorative eggs they may have and indicate from which country they came.

RELATED ACTIVITIES

HIDDEN EGGS. In the sensory table, hide plastic eggs in Easter grass or under sand.

GREEN EGGS AND HAM. Invite parents to a Green Eggs and Ham Party. Here's a recipe for this delicious snack:

1 egg per child	oil or butter
ham, cut up	milk, 1/4 cup
Green food coloring	Chopped spinach (optional)

Have children wash their hands. Each child cracks an egg into a medium size bowl. Pour in milk and a few drops of food coloring. Add the spinach. Let each child cut up the ham with a butter knife. Heat oil or butter in a skillet. Pour in eggs, add ham and scramble while cooking. Serve warm. *KEEP CHILDREN AWAY FROM SKILLET WHILE ADULT COOKS THE EGGS.*

OBSERVE A BIRD. Find someone to bring in a bird for the children to observe for a day or a week. Ask parents, other teachers, or even a pet store to help out.

RELATED MUSIC

Humpty Dumpty
Bluebird Through My Window
Two Little Blackbirds

RELATED LITERATURE

Brown, Margaret Wise. (1943). **THE GOLDEN EGG BOOK**. New York: Western Publishing.

Eastman, P.D. (1960). **ARE YOU MY MOTHER?** New York: Random House.

Heller, Ruth, (1981). **CHICKENS AREN'T THE ONLY ONES.** New York: Grosset and Dunlap.

Heine, Helme (1983). **THE MOST WONDERFUL EGG IN THE WORLD.** New York: Macmillan Publishing Company.

Seuss, Dr.(1960). **GREEN EGGS AND HAM.** New York: Random House.

Seuss, Dr.(1940). **HORTON HATCHES AN EGG.** New York: Random House.

DID YOU FEED MY COW

a call and response song

Well did you feed my cow? *"Yes, ma'am"* (nod head) Well did you

feed my cow? *"Yes. ma'am"* (nod head) Well, what did you feed her?

"Corn and hay," What did you feed her? 1, 2, 3. *spoken* *"Corn and hay."*

4. *spoken* How did they come? *Flop, flop, flop* (Flap arms) *And that was the end of the cow.*

2. Did you milk her good? (*yes, ma'am*)   nod head
   Did you milk her like you should? (*yes, ma'am*)   nod head
   Well, how did you milk her? (*squish, squish, squish*)   make milking motion with hands
   Well, how did you milk her? (*squish, squish, squish*)   make milking motion with hands

3. Did my cow get sick? (*yes, ma'am*)   nod head
   Was she covered with tick? (*yes, ma'am*)   nod head
   Well, how did she die? (*m-m-m*) shake head
   Well, how did she die? (*m-m-m*)   shake head

4. Did the buzzards come? (*yes, ma'am*) nod head
   Did the buzzards come? (*yes, ma'am*) nod head
   Well how did they come? (*flop, flop, flop*) flap arms
   Well how did they come? (*flop, flop, flop*) flap arms

LARGE GROUP TIME

SING IN TWO GROUPS. Divide the class into two groups. One group sings the questions while the other group sings the responses.

EXPLAIN WORDS THEY MAY NOT KNOW. Although adults tend to find this song rather gruesome, children love it. Explain what a tick is and why it might cause the cow to get sick and die.. You will probably also have to explain about a buzzard.

CHANGE WORDS. You can rewrite this song to be about other animals. The children might want to change the ending to be happier, too. Don't forget to write it as questions and answers. Here's an example:

Did you feed my dog? *(yes, ma'am)*
Did you feed my dog? *(yes, ma'am)*
What did you feed her? *(dry dog food)*
What did you feed her? *(dry dog food)*

CURRICULUM INTEGRATION

FARMS
ANIMALS

SCIENCE

ANIMAL FOODS. On the science table, display a selection of foods that animals eat such as corn, hay, grain, cat food, dog food, bird seed.

MAKE BUTTER. Fill baby food jars half full with whipping cream. Screw the lid on tightly. The children shake the jars vigorously for around 10 minutes. It's fun to put on some dancing music while they shake their jars. After the butter forms, pour off the buttermilk and let the children taste the milk. Serve the butter on crackers or bread.

MAKE YOGURT, CHEESE, OR ICE CREAM. Use your favorite recipe and make a dairy product.

MATH

ANIMAL GRAPH. Place pictures of animals at the top of a graph. The children can place a sticky dot below the picture of their favorite animal. Which animal was liked by the most children? Which got the fewest votes?

WHAT'S MISSING? Place 3, 4, or 5 plastic animals or feltboard animals where the children can see. Tell them to memorize where each animal is. Cover the animals with a large scarf or a screen. Remove one animal without the children seeing which one. Take away the screen or scarf and the children guess what's missing.

COUNT BACKWARDS. Place plastic animals or feltboard animals in a row. Count them backwards from 10 to 1 or 5 to 1 depending on the age of the children. Also, practice subtraction by taking one or two animals away and asking the children how many are left.

SORT AND CLASSIFY. Give the children an assortment of plastic animals. They can sort and classify them by color, where they live, types of fur or feathers, ears, feet, etc.

ANIMAL PATTERNS. Place two or three pictures on the flannelboard or use plastic animals to start a pattern. What comes next in the pattern?

ART

THINGS ON A FARM. Cut and glue magazine pictures of things you would find on a farm.

BUTTERMILK CHALK PICTURES. Spread a thin coat of buttermilk or liquid starch on paper with a brush or your hands. Draw on the wet paper with colored chalk.

FINISH THE ANIMAL. Glue one half a picture of a farm animal on a piece of paper. The children can draw the other half. Don't expect children under five to be able to make it look like it should, but they can still have fun with it. Another way to do this is to glue one farm animal on a page and have the children decorate around it.

FARM MURAL. Children can draw or find magazine pictures of farm animals to put on a murals. Farm animal stencils work well, too.

WHOLE LANGUAGE / READING

ANIMAL RHYMES. Using animals names, write some funny rhymes about them with the children. Use your rhyme bank or rhyme cards to make it easier. Here's an example :

How now brown cow?
What's that black cat?
Where's your house, little mouse?

17

"MY FARM" BOOK. Write class or individual books about a farm. Children can write or dictate their ideas about what their farm would be like, what animals, machinery, buildings, crops, etc. would be on it.

ADULT AND BABY ANIMALS. Show pictures or use plastic animals of adult and baby animals. Write the names on chart paper or the chalkboard. You often can find stickers with mother and baby animals that you could use to make matching cards. For beginning readers, the children can match the name with the animal. Non-readers can match the baby animal with its mother.

MULTI-CULTURAL

ANIMALS AROUND THE WORLD. Teach the children the words for animals in another language. If you have a child or parent in your class that speaks another language, enlist their help.

ENGLISH	FRENCH	SPANISH
cow	la vache	la vaca
cat	le chat	el gato
horse	le cheval	el caballo

RELATED ACTIVITIES

VISIT A FARM. If you are fortunate enough to live near a farm, arrange a field trip. Invite parents to go with you.

VISIT A DAIRY. Most cities have a dairy or dairy processing plant that give tours. If they won't give tours, they often have a speaker that will come and talk to your class about how they process milk into cheese, butter, yogurt, ice cream, etc.

DAIRY SNACKTIME. Ask parents to send an assortment of dairy products for snacktime i.e. ice cream, yogurt, cream cheese, cottage cheese, butter, etc. Have crackers for spreading butter and cream cheese.

RELATED MUSIC

BINGO
Farmer in the Dell
Old MacDonald
Baa Baa Black Sheep
Six Little Ducks

RELATED LITERATURE

Brown, Craig. (1991). **MY BARN.** New York: Greenwillow Books.

Rounds, G. (1989). **OLD MACDONALD HAD A FARM.** New York: Holiday House.

Selsam, Millicient. (1967). **ALL KINDS OF BABIES.** New York: Four Winds.

Selsam, Millicient. (1965). **ANIMALS AS PARENTS.** New York: Morrow.

Most, Bernard. (1990). **THE COW THAT WENT OINK.** San Diego: Harcourt, Brace, Jovanovich.

DREIDL SONG

2. It has a lovely body, with legs so short and thin,
   And when it gets all tired, it drops and then I win.

(LARGE GROUP TIME)

SPIN LIKE A DREIDL. If you can get a dreidl, demonstrate to the children how the dreidl spins and then falls. (Call a local synagogue to get a dreidl.) While you sing the song, the children spin around like a dreidl. When you stop singing, all the "dreidls" fall down or sit down. Stop singing at intermittent intervals so that the children have lots of chances to spin and fall. They will love this and will want to do it over and over.

TELL THE STORY OF HANUKKAH. Hanukkah- the Jewish Festival of Lights falls in December. Since the Jewish calendar is a lunar calendar, the date of Hanukkah changes from year to year, but is always in December.

In a nutshell, Hanukkah celebrates the rededication of the Temple in

Jerusalem which the Jewish Soldiers, under the command of Judah Macabee, won back from the Syrians. When they recaptured the Temple, the Jews found only enough oil to keep the eternal flame burning for a day, but miraculously the oil burned for eight days, long enough to make new oil. It is for this reason that Hanukkah is celebrated for eight days. In Jewish homes, a candle on the menorah is lit for each night of Hanukkah. Gifts are exchanged and families play the dreidl game and eat foods fried in oil. Potato latkes are a favorite Hanukkah food.

CURRICULUM INTEGRATION

HANUKKAH
WINTER HOLIDAYS
LIGHT

SCIENCE

THINGS THAT GIVE LIGHT. Show the class a menorah. There are nine candles, but only eight nights of Hanukkah. The candle that is placed higher than the others is called the *shamos* or helper candle. The *shamos* is used to light the other candles. What else can the children think of that gives off light? (flashlights, lightbulbs, lanterns, matches, fireplaces) Bring in a collection of things that give off light, (no matches, please!) and display them on the science table.

THINGS THAT SPIN. Ask the children to bring in things that spin. They might bring in tops, gyroscopes, toy helicopters, airplanes with propellers, globes, etc.

SCIENCE EXPERIMENT. Demonstrate how fire needs oxygen to burn. Set a candle on a plate. Light the candle and cover the candle with a glass jar or a drinking glass. As the candle uses up the oxygen in the cup, the flame will get dimmer until it finally goes out.

MATH

COUNT THE CANDLES. Count the nine candles on the menorah. Light one. How many are left? Light another. Now how many are left? Continue to do this until all are lit. You could light one each day of the eight days of Hanukkah, so that by the eighth day all eight candles plus the *shamos* is lit. The *shamos* is the helper candle that lights all the others.

CANDLES ON A MENORAH. Have children glue cut out candles on a predrawn or cut out menorah. They can place a flame on each candle every day of Hanukkah. This reinforces a one to one correspondence.

PLAY DREIDL. Each player gets five peanuts to begin. Place 10 peanuts in the "pot" in the middle. Depending on which side the dreidl falls, the player either puts in, gets half, gets nothing or gets all. Children under five will need the help of an older student or adult to play this.

ג-*gimmel*- get all in the pot   נ-*nun*-get nothing

ה-*hey*-take 1/2 of pot   שׁ-*shin*-put 2 into pot

ART

BUILD A MENORAH OR CANDLE HOLDER. Children can roll out thick playdough snakes and poke holes with small candles. Let the playdough dry. When dry, the children can decorate the menorahs with paint and glitter. Candle holders and menorahs can be made from a block of wood onto which a clay bead or wooden spool has been glued.

MAKE CANDLES. Purchase candle making supplies at a craft store. You can buy supplies for either dipped candles or candles from a mold, which is easier with young children. Be sure to have an extra adult or two around when making candles since hot wax can be dangerous.

WHOLE LANGUAGE / READING

WORD CHART. Brainstorm things that give light and write the words on chart paper or a chalkboard.

HEBREW LETTERS. Explain that the letters on the dreidl are Hebrew letters. Show the equivalent letter in English:

ג-G-*gimmel*

נ-N-*nun*

שׁ-Sh-*shin*

ה-H-*hey*

MULTI-CULTURAL

WINTER HOLIDAY PROGRAM. If you you doing a winter holiday program, include some Hanukkah songs.

ISRAELI DANCING. Call a synagogue, Jewish Community Center, or university dance department for someone to teach Israeli dances to your class. *Hava Negilah* and *Mayim* are easy dances for young children.

COOK POTATO LATKES. For this traditional Hanukkah food:
Peel and grate 1/2 potato per child, keep rinsing in cold water until all potatoes are peeled and grated. Squeeze out all the excess water. Add one egg and one tablespoon of flour for each 6 potatoes. Add a pinch of salt and pepper. Drop a pancake size scoopful into a frying pan into which you have heated an inch of oil. Fry latkes on both sides until golden brown. Serve topped with sour cream and applesauce.

RELATED MUSIC

Hanukkah, Hanukkah
One Little Candle

RELATED LITERATURE

Adler, David. (1982). Ill. by Linda Heller. **A PICTURE BOOK OF CHANUKAH.** New York: Holiday.

Geliman, Ellie. (1985). Ill. by Katherine J. Cahn. **IT'S CHANUKAH.** Rockville, Md.: Kar Been.

Goffstein, M.B. (1980). **LAUGHING LATKES.** New York: Farrar, Straus and Giroux.

FIVE LITTLE PUMPKINS

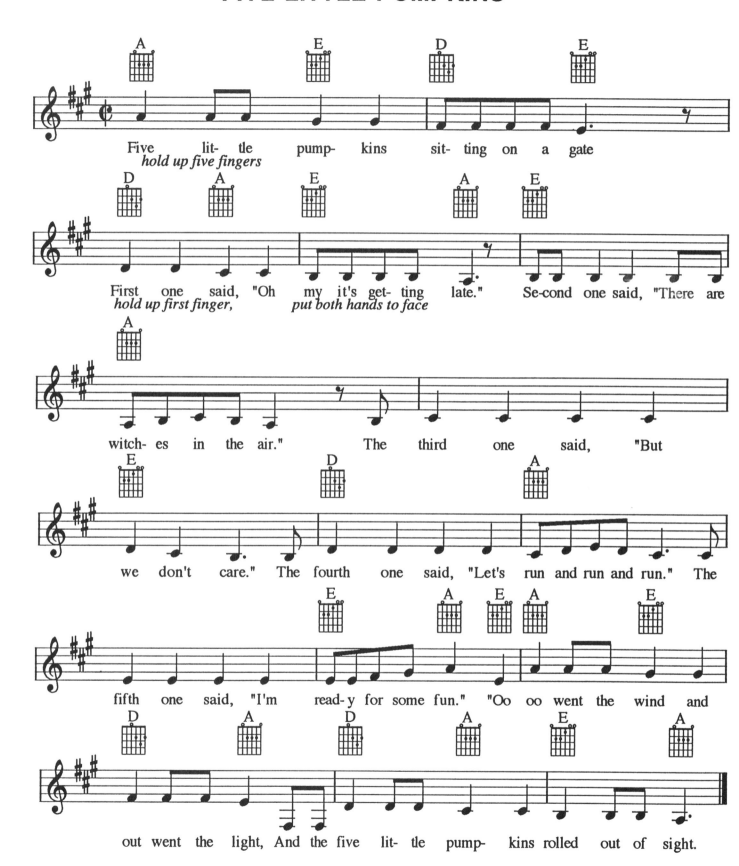

Five lit- tle pump- kins sit- ting on a gate
hold up five fingers

First one said, "Oh my it's get- ting late." Se- cond one said, "There are
hold up first finger, *put both hands to face*

witch- es in the air." The third one said, "But

we don't care." The fourth one said, "Let's run and run and run." The

fifth one said, "I'm read- y for some fun." "Oo oo went the wind and

out went the light, And the five lit- tle pump- kins rolled out of sight.

24

MAKE UP MOTIONS. Children can hold up the appropriate number of fingers and make up motions for each verse.

ACT IT OUT. Pick five children to be the pumpkins. Assign each child a number and he/she acts out the words for that pumpkin. If you have enough room, they can all "roll out of sight," by doing a somersault the the end. If not, have them make a rolling motion with their hands.

"WIGGLE OUT OF SIGHT." Instead of having the five little pumpkins "roll out of sight," have them "wiggle," "hop" or "jump out of sight."

USE PUPPETS. Provide pumpkin puppets make of orange construction paper pumpkins glued to a craft stick. The children hold up one pumpkin puppet at a time as you sing the song.

CURRICULUM INTEGRATION

PUMPKINS / HALLOWEEN
COUNTING

SCIENCE

WHAT'S INSIDE? Before cutting into a pumpkin, ask the children to predict what they think it will be like on the inside. Record their predictions. How will it look, smell, touch, taste? After you cut it open, have the children help scoop it out (encourage them to touch the gooey insides.) When it is all cleaned out, return to their predictions and see if they were correct.

WATCH IT MOLD. Leave a section of raw pumpkin on the science table for a week or two. It will shrivel up and then mold will grow on it. Provide magnifying glasses for observing and paper and pencil for recording the changes.

PLANT PUMPKIN SEEDS. Dry out the pumpkin seeds you scooped out. The children can plant them in a plastic zip top bag in a variety of medium such as wet cotton, soil, sand, wet paper towel. Tape the bags to a window and observe what happens. Discuss which grew best, slowest, fastest, not at all. Why do they think they got these results?

BAKE IT. You can bake or boil sections of pumpkin and scoop out the pulp. Make pumpkin pie or pumpkin bread. Let the children taste the pumpkin raw, cooked with no sugar, cooked with sugar, and baked.

MATH

FLANNELBOARD PUMPKINS. Place five felt pumpkins on the flannelboard. Remove the pumpkins one by one and have the children figure out how many are left.

GUESS THE CIRCUMFERENCE. Bring in one or two pumpkins of different sizes. The children can "guesstimate" the circumference of the pumpkin by cutting a piece of string they think will fit around its middle. After each child has cut his/her piece of string, they can try to fit it around the middle. Is it too long, too short, or just right? Make a chart with three sections that say "too short," "too long," and "just right.'' The children can place their strings in the appropriate section. Count up how many strings are in each section.

GROUPS OF FIVE. Sort beans, bottletops, or pumpkin seeds into groups of five. Count the groups of five to see how many there are all together.

MATCH THE JACK-O-LANTERN. Create five different matching pairs of jack-o-lanterns for the flannelboard. Place the pairs on the flannelboard in random order and have the children pick out the matching pairs.

ART

JACK-O-LANTERN FACE. Provide the students with orange pumpkin shape cut-outs onto which they can glue black geometric shapes for eyes, nose and mouth.

PAINT A PUMPKIN. Cut out large pumpkin shapes for easel paper and put out green, orange and black paint.

PUMPKIN SEED COLLAGE. Save the pumpkin seeds you scooped out of the pumpkin. Let them dry out and glue them onto paper for a collage.

SPONGE PAINTING. You can purchase jack-o-lantern shaped sponges at craft stores or cut out the shapes from kitchen sponges. Children can dip them in a shallow pan of orange tempera and stamp them on paper.

WHOLE LANGUAGE / READING

WORD CHART. Ask the children to brainstorm all the things they can think of that have to do with Halloween. Write their ideas on the board or on chart paper.

"FIVE LITTLE PUMPKINS" BOOK. You can preprint the words on each page for three, four, and five year olds. The children can either draw their own pumpkins, they can glue pumpkins shapes, or stamp pumpkins on each page.

RELATED ACTIVITIES

VISIT A PUMPKIN PATCH. If you are fortunate enough to know someone with a pumpkin patch, take the class to pick out their own pumpkins. Invite parents to join your field trip.

FIND A PUMPKIN. Take a class trip to the supermarket in order for each child to pick out their own. It's also fun to buy pumpkins ahead of time (many supermarkets will donate them) and hide them around the school grounds for pumpkin hunt.

PUMPKIN CUT-UP. Provide "pumpkin knives" that can be purchased at grocery stores around Halloween and pieces of pumpkin. The children can cut up the pumpkin . Some children will want to stay at this activity all day.

RELATED MUSIC

Skin and Bones
Three Little Witches
Eentsy Weentsy Spider

RELATED LITERATURE

Bridwell, Norman. (1970). **CLIFFORD'S HALLOWEEN.** New York: Scholastic.

Johnston, Tony. (1983). **THE VANISHING PUMPKIN.** Toronto: General Publishing Company.

Miller, Edna. (1964). **MOUSEKINS GOLDEN HOUSE.** Canada: Prentice-Hall.

Titherington, Jeanne. (1986). **PUMPKIN, PUMPKIN.** New York: Greenwillow.

Williams, Linda. (1986).**THE LITTLE OLD LADY WHO WASN'T AFRAID OF ANYTHING.** New York: Crowell.

HUSH LITTLE BABY

Hush lit-tle ba- by don't say a word. Pa-pa's gon-na buy you a mock-ing bird. And if that mock-ing- bird won't sing, Pa- pa's gon-na buy you a dia- mond ring.

2. If that diamond ring turns brass, Papa's gonna buy you a looking glass.
3. If that looking glass gets broke, Papa's gonna buy you a billy goat.
4. If that billy goat don't pull, Papa's gonna buy you a cart and bull.
5. If that cart and bull turn over, Papa's gonna buy you a dog named Rover.
6. If that dog named Rover don't bark, Papa's gonna buy you a horse and cart.
7. If that horse and cart fall down, you'll still be the sweetest little baby in town.

(LARGE GROUP TIME)

MOMMA'S GONNA BUY. Change the words "Papa's gonna buy" to "Momma's gonna buy,". You can also sing about Grandma and Grandpa.

ACT IT OUT. Get together small toys and props to act this out. Replace the words "baby" and "Papa" with the names of students in your class. The child whose acting as "Papa" can give the prop to the child who is replacing the baby:

> Hush little David don't say a word,
> Lindsey's gonna buy you a mockingbird...

FLANNELBOARD PICTURES. Prepare pictures of the things in the song for the flannelboard. Give the pictures to the children and as you sing the song, have the children put the pictures up in the correct order.

CHANGE THE WORDS. Leave off the last words and have the children make up new words. It might be helpful to use your rhyme bank or rhyme cards in making up verses.

> Hush little baby, don't say a word, Papa's gonna buy you a mockingbird;
> If that mockingbird don't fly, Papa's gonna buy you a cherry pie;
> If that cherry pie's not sweet, Papa's gonna buy you some candy to eat...

29

FAMILIES
BABIES

SCIENCE

BABY FOOD AND BIG KIDS' FOOD. Let the children taste a variety of foods prepared as baby food and in the way they usually eat it. They can try pureed bananas, carrots, peas and then the same foods in the raw and/or cooked form.

BABY ANIMALS. Animal babies are often called something different than their mom and dad. Show pictures of animal mothers and babies and talk about their names:

cow-calf	goat-kid	pig-piglet	horse-foal
kangaroo-joey	duck-duckling	owl- owlet	swan-cygnet

MATH

COUNTING. Count how many things Papa's gonna buy.

WHEN YOU WERE A BABY. Ask children to bring in clothing from when they were babies and toddlers. Compare the sizes and have the children guess how old they might have been when they wore that item.

FAMILY GRAPH. Make a graph with the numbers or number representation for 2,3,4,5,6 or more. Count the number of people who live in each child's household and mark in it the appropriate column. How many children have 2 people living in their house, how many have 3,4,5? Whose family is the biggest? Whose is the smallest?

ART

FAMILY TREE. Draw a tree with branches on construction paper. Ask children to bring in family photos that will be glued onto a family tree. Children can glue the photos on the branches of the tree.

DOLL CRADLES. Take an empty oatmeal box and cut through it half way length-wise. Children can decorate it and line it with fabric for a blanket.

DOLL BLANKETS. Cut doll blankets from flannel, old sheets or old blankets. The children can decorate them with fabric, crayons or felt tip pens.

PICTURES OF BABIES. Children can look through magazines for pictures of babies that they can cut out and glue on paper.

WHOLE LANGUAGE / READING

WORD CHART. What do families do together? Write the children's responses on chart paper or the chalkboard.

"HUSH LITTLE BABY" BOOK. Create a class book with new verses the children have written. The children can illustrate the pages by drawing pictures or by looking for magazine cut outs of the things Papa's gonna buy.

FAMILY ALBUM. Put together a family album for each child. You can either use photographs that the family sends in or the children can draw pictures of each family member and dictate or write a short sentence about each person.

MULTI-CULTURAL

BABIES AROUND THE WORLD. Look through magazines and books to get a collection of pictures of babies from different countries and ethnic backgrounds. Perhaps you can find pictures of the many ways mothers around the world transport their babies and of the different types of cribs and cradles used. Talk about what is the same and what is different from where they live.

RELATED ACTIVITIES

FAMILY DAY. Each month have a "Family Day" where one or two children invite a family member(s) to bring a special activity to the class. They could do a cooking project, read a story, sing a song, build something, play an instrument, etc.

BATHING BABY DOLLS. During free choice time provide plastic baby dolls win a plastic tub for the children to wash. have lots of towels available.

OBSERVE A REAL BABY. Invite a mom or dad and their baby to visit the classroom. Talk about how the baby is different than they are and how the baby is the same?

SNACKTIME. Serve a variety of baby foods for snacktime.

RELATED MUSIC

Miss Lucy
Rock-a-bye Baby
Baby Beluga (by Raffi)
Sleep, Baby, Sleep
Fais Dodo

RELATED LITERATURE

Alexander, Martha. (1971). **NOBODY ASKED IF I WANTED A BABY SISTER.** New York: Dial Press.

Aliki. (1968). **HUSH LITTLE BABY.** Canada: Prentice-Hall.

Eastman, P.D. (1960). **ARE YOU MY MOTHER?** New York: Random House.

Jonas, Ann. (1982). **WHEN YOU WERE A BABY.** New York: Greenwillow.

Keats, Ezra Jack. (1967). **PETER'S CHAIR.** New York: Harper.

Wood, Audrey. (1984). Ill. by Don Wood. **THE NAPPING HOUSE.** New York: Harcourt.

I'M ME, I'M SPECIAL

by Stephanie Burton

33

LARGE GROUP TIME

MAKE UP MOTIONS. Ask the children to help you make up motions for this song.

HOLDING HANDS. With children all sitting or standing in a circle, they can hold hands and gently sway while singing.

WHO'S SPECIAL TODAY? Each day pick a different child about whom to sing either the the whole song or just one verse:
    Julianna, she's special
    There's no one else that's just like her...

CURRICULUM INTEGRATION

ALL ABOUT ME

SCIENCE

MIRRORS. Provide mirrors and magnifying glasses of various sizes for the children to examine their features, skin and clothing.

WHO'S THAT TALKING? Tape record the children's voices while talking, singing and playing. Let them listen to themselves and guess whose voice they hear.

VIDEO TAPE. While the children are working or playing, video tape them. Play it the same day or the next day and watch the children's faces as they watch themselves on T.V.

MATH

SAME AND DIFFERENT. Have the children look at each other and compare what is the same and different about each other.

COUNT HOW MANY. Count how many children in the room have similar characteristics i.e. hair color, eye color, clothing, etc.

HANDPRINT SIZE. Make handprints or footprints by tracing the children's hands or feet. Compare the different sizes and shapes. If you make two handprints or footprints of each child, they can use them for a matching game.

FRAME ME. Take a photo of each child. Cut rectangles or circles on which to mount each photo. Provide markers with which children can decorate the "frame."

SELF-PORTRAITS. Children that are doing representational drawing can draw or paint self-portraits or portraits of another child in the class. Supply the children with skin-tone crayons or paints which are available from educational supply catalogs or stores.

COOPERATIVE BODY TRACING. On a body-size sheet of butcher paper, have each child lay down while you trace one part of his/her body. When you've finished, you'll have Tony's arm, Nikki's leg, Ann's head, etc. The children can paint or color the body tracing .

WHOLE LANGUAGE / READING

MAKE YOUR OWN "IMPORTANT BOOK." Read "The Important Book" to the class. Create your own "Important Book" by asking each child what is important about them. Each child will have his/her own page. Glue a photo of the child on their page and they can illustrate around it by painting, drawing or cutting and gluing a magazine cut-out. For example:
> The important thing about Joshua is... he loves baseball.
> The important thing about Lindsey is...she plays piano.

Send your "Important Book" home with a different child each week to share with their parents. Put a few blank sheets at the end on which parents can write comments.

"ALL ABOUT ME" BOOK. Children can work on this book throughout the year. Include drawings the child has made and photos of the child at school and home. They can draw or cut out magazine pictures of their favorite food, toys, animals, activities, etc.

MULTI-CULTURAL

WHAT MAKES UP SPECIAL. Talk about how each child is different and that's what makes them so special. Compare the children's hair color and texture, skin color, eye color, and height. What do they think it would be like if we all looked the same?

MULTI-CULTURAL CLASSROOM. Be sure to have dolls, books, games, music and kitchen equipment available that represent the various races and ethnic backgrounds of the children in your class.

RELATED ACTIVITIES

STAR OF THE WEEK. Set up a permanent bulletin board featuring a different child each week. Send home a questionnaire for parents to fill out about where the child was born, favorite foods, toys, activities, how many people live with the child. Post the questionnaire and photos of the child on the board for the week. The featured child can wear a star button or necklace each day that week.

RELATED MUSIC

If You're Happy and You Know It
The More We Get Together

RELATED LITERATURE

Carlson, Nancy. (1988). **I LIKE ME. New York:** Viking Kestrel.

Brown, Margaret Wise.(1949).**THE IMPORTANT BOOK.** NewYork: Harper and Row.

Hines, Anna Grossnickle. (1985). **ALL BY MYSELF.** New York; Clarion.

Martin, Bill, Jr. and Archambault, John. (1987). Illustrated by Ted Rand. **HERE ARE MY HANDS.** New York: Henry Holt and Company.

JINGLE BELLS

NAME THAT TUNE. Introduce this song by humming the melody and see who can guess what song it is.

ONE HORSE OPEN SLEIGH. Children love to sing this song, but most little ones have no idea what the song is about. Show a picture of a sleigh and discuss its use as a form of transportation before there were automobiles. What do they think it would feel like to "dash through the snow in a one horse open sleigh." What could they do to stay warm since there is no heater and it may be snowing? The words "bells on bobtail ring," are about the bells around the neck of a horse whose tail has been "bobbed" or shortened.

PLAY BELLS. Give each child bells to play during this song. Explain that the jingle bells were placed around the horse's neck that was pulling a sleigh. When the horse moved, the bells jingled. Jingle bells can be purchased at most hobby and craft stores. You can string a few on a piece of elastic which you can make into a bracelet. Different types of bells can be purchased from teacher supply catalogs.

CURRICULUM INTEGRATION

CHRISTMAS
WINTER

SCIENCE

BELL DISPLAY. Ask children to bring in different types of bells. Set them up as a display. What other kinds of bells can the children think of ? (Church bells, fire bells, school bells, dinner bells)

SOUND BINGO. There are several Sound Bingo games available commercially or you can make your own. On a tape recorder, record several familiar sounds such as brushing teeth, piano playing, vacuuming, car starting, laughter, dog barking. Create your own Bingo cards by drawing pictures of the sounds you recorded on a grid. Copy the card several times, cut up the pictures, and reglue them on a new piece of paper in a different order each time so that each child's Bingo card looks different. Give each child beans to mark the picture of the sound that he/she hears on the recording. The first child to cover the entire card yells, "BINGO!" With children under 5, continue to play so that each child gets a "Bingo."

BELL GUESSING GAME. Gather together a few bells that sound different. Place a color dot or shape sign on each bell as a way to identify them. Play each bell for the children so that they can see which bell makes what sound. Next, play the bell behind a partition so that the children can hear the bell but cannot see it. See if they can guess which bell you played.

SPOON CHIMES. Tie two spoons 3 to 4 inches apart in the middle of a long string. Have a child hold the ends of the strings against their ears, lean forward and gently sway so that the spoons bang together. It should sound like church bells as the sound travels up the string.

(MATH)

TOY STORE. Set up a "toy store" in which children can pretend to purchase toys. For children four and over, you can put price tags on items and give them pretend money with which to make their purchases. At the end of the session, the toys can be placed back on the toy store shelves.

BELL MATH. Purchase small jingle bells at a craft shop and have children count, sort, add and subtract with them.

STRINGING BELLS. Children can string bells on a lace. They can count them and compare who has the most, the fewest, the same. Have them listen to the sounds the bells make. Which makes a louder sound, the lace with the most bells, or the lace with the fewest bells?

MATCHING BELLS. Cut out bells of different colors, sizes or patterns. Children can match them, sort them, seriate them or make patterns with them.

(ART)

DOOR CHIME. Glue jingle bells onto a long strip of red or green felt into which a slit has been made to slip over a door knob.

JINGLE BELL NECKLACE. Children can string a jingle bell along with colored macaroni to make a necklace.

BELL ORNAMENTS. Cut an egg carton into segments to resemble bells. The children can decorate them with glue, glitter, bits of crumpled tissue paper, macaroni or other collage materials. You can attach a jingle bell to the inside of the bell by inserting a pipecleaner through a hole in the middle of the top.

39

SYMBOLS OF CHRISTMAS. Brainstorm Christmas symbols and write them on the board or on chart paper. Ideas might include snow, lights, Christmas trees, Rudolph, Santa.

HOLIDAY STORY. Have the children write a story about their favorite thing to do during the holidays. Be sensitive to the fact that some families in your class may not celebrate Christmas. Invite parents of children who do not celebrate Christmas to come into the classroom and share some of their holiday with the children.

MULTI-CULTURAL

WINTER HOLIDAYS AROUND THE WORLD. Just about every culture, religion or ethnic group has a celebration in the winter. Ask parents and grandparents to share their ethnic diversity with the class by bringing some part of their holiday to discuss or demonstrate.
Here are a few ideas:

Hanukkah- For this Jewish holiday, play dreidl, make latkes, look at a Menorah, count to ten in Hebrew. (See Dreidl Song)

Kwanzaa- This African-American holiday starts December 26 and lasts seven days. Make a friendship chain using red, green and black, the colors of the African flag, count to ten in Swahili, make a woven mat using the colors of the African flag.

St. Lucia's Day- This is celebrated Dec. 13 in several European countries. In Sweden girls wear a white dress with a red sash and a crown of evergreens in which are placed glowing candles. They serve coffee and sweet twisted buns. You can make "Lucia Buns" by using frozen bread dough and twisting it into shapes.

Mexico- break a pinata which you have filled with candy or small toys. Ask parents to donate old fast food toys for toys.

China- decorate a Tree of Life with paper lanterns.

RELATED ACTIVITIES

BAKE COOKIES. Have the children deliver plates of cookies to staff members who are special to them.

SLEIGH RIDE. If you are lucky enough to live near someplace that offers sleigh rides, arrange a field trip. Invite parents to come along. To find a place that may do this, look in the phone book, call you local visitor's center, or contact a horse stable for information.

CANNED GOODS FOR NEEDY FAMILIES. Ask families to bring in canned goods that you can donate to your community food bank or to needy families you may know who would accept a donation.

RELATED MUSIC

Rudolf the Red-Nose Reindeer
Up on the Housetop
Santa Claus is Coming to Town

note: If you are teaching in a public school check on their policy regarding Christmas carols or Christmas celebrations in the classroom.

RELATED LITERATURE

Bemelmans, Ludwing. (1985). **MADELINE'S CHRISTMAS.** New York: Viking.

de Paola, Tomie. (1986). **MERRY CHRISTMAS, STREGA NONA.** New York: Harcourt.

Holabird, Katherine. (1986). **ANGELINA'S CHRISTMAS.** London, Aurum.

Van Allsburg, Chris. (1985). **THE POLAR EXPRESS.** New York: Houghton Mifflin.

MISS LUCY HAD A BABY

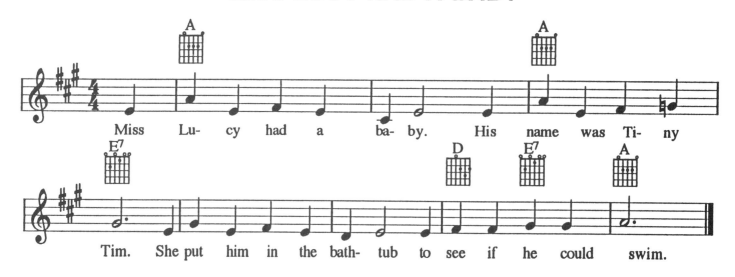

Miss Lu- cy had a ba- by. His name was Ti- ny
Tim. She put him in the bath- tub to see if he could swim.

2. He drank up all the water,
   He ate up all the soap,
   He tried to eat the bathtub
   But it wouldn't go down his throat.

3. Miss Lucy called the doctor,
   Miss Lucy called the nurse,
   Miss Lucy called the lady
   With the alligator purse.

4. "Measles," said the doctor,
   "Mumps," said the nurse,
   "Chickenpox," said the lady
   With the alligator purse.

5. "Penicillin," said the doctor,
   "Penicillin," said the nurse,
   "Penicillin," said the lady
   With the alligator purse.

6. "I don't want the doctor,
   I don't want the nurse,
   I don't want the lady
   With the alligator purse.

7. Out walked the doctor,
   Out walked the nurse,
   Out walked the lady
   With the alligator purse.

(LARGE GROUP TIME)

AMY HAD A BABY. Sing a child's name instead of "Miss Lucy." Each child whose name you use can hold a baby doll or, if he or she prefers, a stuffed animal.

JUMP ROPE. This song is an old and favorite jump rope song. If your students are under five years old you may want to have them just jump from side to side over a rope placed on the floor or over a rope that's gently swaying a few inches above the ground.

CLAPPING HANDS. "Miss Lucy" is also a favorite clapping song. Three and young four year olds can clap their own hands or sit facing a partner and clap their partner's two hands. You can have older children try more difficult clapping patterns:

> * Clap own hands, Clap partner's hands, Clap own hands
> * Pat knees, Clap own hands, Clap partner's hands, Clap own hands.

ACT IT OUT. Choose a child to play each of the parts of Miss Lucy, the doctor, the nurse and the lady (or man) with the alligator purse. The children will want to do this over and over again if you use props:

> Miss Lucy- a hat, or fancy dress or coat
> Tiny Tim- a jar of bubbles to blow bubbles and a box for a bathtub
> Doctor- a doctor bag or stethoscope
> Nurse- a nurse's hat or stethoscope
> Lady with the alligator purse- purse or tote bag

CURRICULUM INTEGRATION

COMMUNITY HELPERS
BUBBLES
BABIES
WATER

SCIENCE

DOCTOR OR NURSE VISIT. Invite a doctor or a nurse to visit the class and talk about their jobs. Arrange for the children to listen to their own heart with the stethoscope, try on a blood pressure cuff and look into someone's ears and eyes with an otoscope.

PURCHASE A STETHOSCOPE. You can purchase a real stethoscope for the class to use from several educational supply catalogs. They cost less than $10.00.

WATER EXPLORATION. Fill the sensory table with water for water exploration. Include pitchers and containers of different sizes and sink or float items,

BUBBLE FUN. Provide bubble solution either in individual containers or in the sensory table. Use a variety of equipment for blowing bubbles such as wands, six ring pop can holders, canning jar rings, etc. Here's a good bubble recipe:

> Mix together 8 Tablespoons liquid dish detergent (Dawn® works best), with 1 quart of water and 1 Tablespoon of glycerin (available in the pharmacy.)

Talk about what makes bubbles. Where else might you find bubbles? Does it work best to blow hard or gently to make the bubbles? Why?

(MATH)

PREDICTING WATER VOLUME. Show the children a container and ask them to predict how many cups of water it will take to fill it. As they help to fill the containers, record how many cups it takes, then compare actual quantities with predicted amounts. Try predicting with pint, quart and gallon size containers. To do this as a small group activity, recruit students in the upper grades or ask parents and grandparents to come in to help.

TINY TIM'S BATHTUB. Get a baby bathtub or use different sized flat, shallow containers and count how many cups, gallons or pints of water it takes to fill it. Bring in baby dolls of various sizes. Have the children predict which dolls will fit in the tub and which won't. Try out their predictions. The children can then wash the babies.

(ART)

BUBBLE ART. In small bowls, add a small amount of tempera to bubble solution. Provide a straw for each child to blow bubbles in his/her bowl. As the bubbles rise above the bowl, lay a piece of white paper on top of the bubbles. As the bubbles pop their outline will be left on the paper.

TONGUE DEPRESSOR STRUCTURES. Ask a physician for a box of tongue depressors and children can construct a building by gluing them together. If you can't find tongue depressors, use craft sticks or popsicle sticks. They can also make pictures by gluing them on construction paper.

DOCTOR SUPPLY COLLAGE. Create a collage using bandage strips, cotton balls, tongue depressors, and gauze tape. You could use paper cut out in the shape of Tiny Tim and the children could doctor him with the collage materials.

BUBBLE PRINTS. Cover the table with bubble wrapping paper available through the post office or office supply stores. The child paints the bubbles with tempera then places construction paper on top of the painted bubbles. Gently lift off the construction paper to reveal a print of the bubble wrap.

WHOLE LANGUAGE / READING

WORD CHART. On the chalkboard or chart paper, write the headings "Babies" and "Five Year Olds" (or the age of your students). Ask the children to tell you what babies do and what children their age can do. Record their responses under the heading.

GROWING UP. Children can create books about themselves as they've grown up. It can include pages such as:
  When I was a little baby...
  When I was one...
  When I was two...
Go up to the child's present age and add:
  Now that I'm (five), I can...
Children can illustrate the pages and/or you can ask parents to send in photos of the child at each age to place in the book. Have the parents write the child's age in each photo on the back of the photo so you'll know on which page it goes.

BUBBLE ADVENTURES. Write a class book about the adventures of a bubble. The children can give the bubbles a name, tell you where the bubble went, what it saw, what was it's biggest worry, who it met, and what happened to the bubble at the end of the story.

MULTI-CULTURAL

BABIES AROUND THE WORLD. Show photos of babies or children from around the world. Discuss how they are the same or different.

RELATED ACTIVITIES

DOCTOR'S OFFICE. Set up a doctor's office in the classroom with a waiting area and examining room. Have at least two doctor's bags with supplies available for sharing.

TINY TIM'S BATHTUB. The sensory table can be set up as a bathtub for washing baby dolls. Have washcloths and towels available.

BUBBLE JUMP. Give each child a piece of plastic bubble wrap. Place it on the floor and let them jump on the bubbles to pop them.

BABY MEMORIES. Each child can bring in an item from when they were a baby. Show them at circle time and then put them on a bulletin board display called "See How We've Grown!"

BANDAGE FUN. Children love to play with bandages and bandage strips. Ask parents to send in boxes of bandages for the children to use to play doctor on stuffed animals, baby dolls and themselves.

DOCTOR KITS. Children can make simple doctor kits by folding in half an 8 1/2 x 11 inch piece of paper and stapling or taping on the two sides. Attach a handle of yarn or string. Children can decorate it and then fill it with bandage strips, gauze, tongue depressors, and cotton balls.

RELATED MUSIC

Miss Polly Had a Dolly
What Shall We Do With the Baby-O?
Doctor Knickerbocker
Bathtime (by Raffi)

RELATED LITERATURE

Meyer, Mercer. (1973). **BUBBLES, BUBBLES.** Troll : New York.

Miller, Margaret. (1988). **WHOSE HAT?** New York: Greenwillow.

Rey, H.A. (1966). **CURIOUS GEORGE GOES TO THE HOSPITAL.** Boston: Houghton Mifflin.

Scarry, Richard. (1972). **NICKY GOES TO THE DOCTOR.** New York: Western Publishing.

Westcott, Nadine. (1988). **THE LADY WITH THE ALLIGATOR PURSE.** Boston: Little, Brown.

Wood, Audrey. (1985). Ill. by Don Wood. **KING BIDGOOD IN THE BATHTUB.** San Diego: Harcourt, Brace, Jovanovich.

MISS MARY MACK

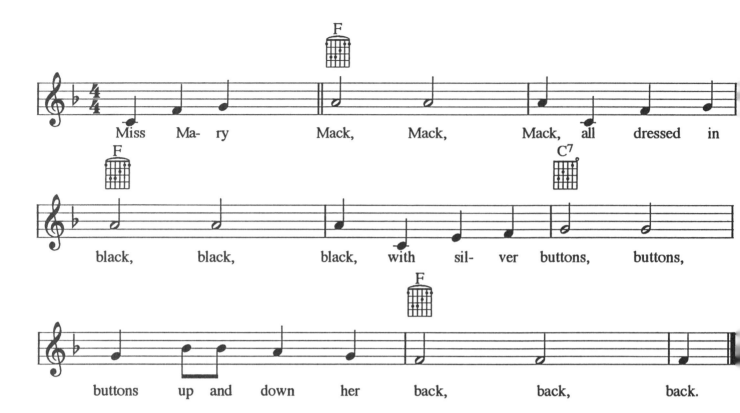

2. She asked her mother, mother, mother,
   For fifteen cents, cents, cents,
   To watch the elephants, elephants, elephants,
   Jump the fence, fence, fence.

3. They jumped so high, high, high,
   They reached the sky, sky, sky,
   And they didn't come back, back, back,
   Til the fourth of July, July, July.

(LARGE GROUP TIME)

CLAPPING PATTERNS. You can make up your own clapping pattern
depending on the abilities of your students. Children three and four years
old may do well simply clapping their own hands on the repeating word at
the end of each phrase:

Mack, Mack, Mack   Black, black, black
Buttons, buttons, buttons   Back, back, back

Older children might enjoy clapping patterns where they clap their own
hands, then clap their friend's hands. Think back to some clapping patterns
you may have used as a child or ask the children if they can make up one to
demonstrate.

PLAY INSTRUMENTS. Instead of singing the repeating words, have
them play instruments where the words should be.

CALL AND RESPONSE SINGING. The teacher can sing the first words of each line and the children can respond by singing the repeating words:

Teacher: Miss Mary   *Children:* Mack, Mack, Mack
Teacher: All dressed in   *Children:* black, black, black

MISS MARY LOU DRESSED IN BLUE. Ask the children what other colors Miss Mary might wear and write new verses:

Miss Mary Lou, Lou, Lou,
All dressed in blue, blue, blue,
With silver buckles, buckles, buckles,
Up and down her shoe, shoe, shoe.

CURRICULUM INTEGRATION

COLORS
ANIMALS
ZOO
CIRCUS
ELEPHANTS

SCIENCE

BUTTON HUMMERS. Take a large button and pull a piece of string through two holes. Tie the string at one end. Slide the button to the middle of the string and place each of the two loops over each hand. Twist the string and then spin the button by pulling inward and outward with your hands. The button will hum as it winds and unwinds.

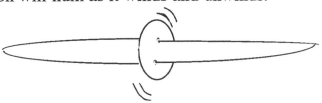

STUDY ELEPHANTS. Ask your local library for books and magazines about elephants. Share them with your class. Each day discuss a unique aspect of the elephant. Could an elephant jump over a fence? Could it "jump so high to reach the sky?"

MATH

BUTTON SORTING. Gather buttons of various sizes, shapes, colors, and textures for the children to sort and classify. Ask the families in your class to donate buttons or you can buy an assortment at hobby shops for under $10.

HOW FAR CAN YOU JUMP? Measure how far each child can jump. You can measure using inches, connecting links, or blocks lined end to end. Graph the results on a large graph. Compare the results. Who jumped the farthest, the shortest, the same?

HOW MUCH IS FIFTEEN? Miss Mary Mack asked her mother for fifteen cents. What does that look like in pennies? How else can we show fifteen cents? Ask the children to bring in fifteen items of one kind from home and make a "15" display. They could bring in 15 bottle caps, 15 corks, 15 marbles, etc.

FIFTEEN CENT STORE. Have a class store where everything costs fifteen cents. You can provide the children with real or pretend money with which to purchase the items.

(ART)

SEWING BUTTONS. Cut a square of burlap for each child. Using embroidery floss, dental floss, or yarn and tapestry needles, the children can practice sewing. Have buttons and beads available to make the project more interesting. Children five and older might enjoy drawing a picture on the burlap first and then following the outline with the yarn. Children who have never sewn before may need help understanding how to take the needle from one side to the other to avoid looping it over the outside.

BLACK COLLAGE. Put out an assortment of black items with which the children can create a collage on paper, wood, foam trays, or paper plates.

MISS MARY MACK. Provide a cut out of a girl to represent Miss Mary Mack. The children can paint her dress black or glue black scraps of paper on her dress. You can use aluminum foil balls for the silver buttons.

(WHOLE LANGUAGE / READING)

MISS MARY MACK CONTINUED. Ask the children what happened next after Miss Mary Mack came back on the Fourth of July. Use the same form as the song repeating the last word of each phrase three times:

> She went back home, home, home,
> To use the phone, phone, phone, phone,
> Since no one was there, there, there,
> She ate an ice cream cone, cone, cone.

POCKET CHART. Write the words on sentence strips and place them in a pocket chart. Ask the children to find the words that are the same to place at the end of each phrase:(for five, six and seven year olds)

| Miss | Mary | Mack | Mack | Mack |

| All | dressed | in | black | black | black |

WORD REPETITION STORY. Write a story with the class using word repetition. It can be about anything the class decides:

    Lindsey likes pizza, pizza, pizza.
    Josh likes ice cream, cream, cream.
    Julianna likes corn, corn, corn.
    Jessica likes peas, peas, peas.

MULTI-CULTURAL

ELEPHANTS AROUND THE WORLD. Elephants are still used as transportation in other countries such as India and Africa. Go to the library and find some illustrations and photographs depicting elephants at work and in the wild.

RELATED ACTIVITIES

BUTTON, BUTTON, WHO'S GOT THE BUTTON? Play this popular game by picking one child to leave the room while you give the button to a child in the room. Every child in the room, including the child who has the button, makes a fist with their hand and puts their hands behind their backs pretending they have the button. The child who left the room comes back in and tries to guess who actually has the button in his/her hand. As he/she walks back into the room, the children chant, "Button, button, who has the button?"

VISIT AN ELEPHANT. Go to the zoo or a circus to see an elephant. Talk about its size, how it moves, the size of its ears and feet, how it uses its trunk.

WALK LIKE AN ELEPHANT. How many different ways can they think of to move like an elephant? If you can find a recording of "Baby Elephant Walk" play it while the children move like elephants. The can dance in pairs, trios, or as an entire group. One child may want to pretend to be an elephant trainer and another child the performing elephant.

JUMP THE FENCE. Build a fence out of cardboard or wood blocks. A child pretends to be an elephant and jumps over the fence. Add blocks and continue jumping until the fence is knocked down.

(RELATED MUSIC)

One Elephant Went Out To Play
Baby Elephant Walk (instrumental)
Mary's Wearing A Red Dress
Going To the Zoo (by Tom Paxton)

(RELATED LITERATURE)

deBrunoff, Laurent. **BABAR** (there are many Babar books)

Freeman, Don. (1968). **CORDUROY.** New York: Viking.

Smith, Jerry.(1979.) **BUT NO ELEPHANTS.** New York: Parents Magazine Press.

Seuss, Dr.(1940.) **HORTON HATCHES THE EGG.** New York: Random House.

Wildsmith, Brian. (1970). **CIRCUS.** New York: Franklin Watts.

THE MULBERRY BUSH

Here we go 'round the mul-ber-ry bush, the mul-ber-ry bush, the mul-ber-ry bush. Here we go 'round the mul-ber-ry bush so ear-ly in__ the morn-ing.

1. This is the way we wash our face..
2. Comb our hair...
3. Brush our teeth...
4. Put on our clothes...
5. Etc.

Children join hands and walk in a circle on the chorus.
They pantomime motions for the verses.

(LARGE GROUP TIME)

GETTING READY FOR SCHOOL. Ask the children what they do to get ready for school. Put their ideas into sequence for new verses and have them make up motions.

SKIP 'ROUND THE MULBERRY BUSH. Instead of "Here we go 'round," sing, "Here we skip (or jump, skate, hop) 'round the mulberry bush." The children move around the circle as the words dictate.

USE A CHILD'S NAME. Ask a child what he or she likes to do at home that they can pantomime. Sing about the child while he/she does the motions:

> Sheila likes to sweep the floor...

OTHER THEME UNITS. This song can be adapted to many different theme units. Start the children with an idea such as planting seeds, or working on a farm, and let them come up with the verses.

CURRICULUM INTEGRATION

COMING TO SCHOOL
PLANTING / SPRINGTIME
HEALTH / HYGIENE
SAFETY

SCIENCE

WHAT IS A MULBERRY BUSH? Chances are that no on in your class has ever seen a mulberry bush. Ask the children if they know what it is. Explain that it is a bush that has red berries.

TREE OR BUSH? What is the difference between a tree or a bush? A bush is a low, branchy plant also known as a shrub. A tree is much taller than a bush and has a single trunk rather than several stems like a bush. Go outside and decide which plants are trees and which are bushes.

KEEPING HEALTHY. Why should you wash your face, brush you teeth, etc.? Talk about the importance of good hygiene and how washing your body regularly rids your body of bad germs. You might want to invite a nurse or doctor in to talk about hand washing and other hygiene issues.

MATH

WEIGH AND MEASURE. At the beginning of the year and periodically thereafter, weigh and measure the children. Record it on a graph or wall chart where the children can see how much they've grown.

HEALTHY PUZZLES. Create puzzles out of pictures of health products i.e. soap, shampoo, toothpaste. Mount magazine photos or product boxes on tagboard and cut zigzags for a puzzle. The number of pieces depends on the children's age.

ART

TOOTHBRUSH PAINTING. Children dip old toothbrushes in paint and brush it on paper. Children can experiment with up and down strokes and a circular brushing motion.

SOAPBALLS. Add enough water to soap flakes to make it easy to mold. You can also add some food coloring for color or some perfume or cologne for scent. Mold it into balls or shapes and let dry. Children can take them home to use in the tub or give as gifts.

WHOLE LANGUAGE / READING

HEALTHY HABITS CHART. Brainstorm ideas that promote good health habits. Write their ideas on chart paper or the board.

ACTIVITY CARDS. Prepare picture cards depicting activities such as washing hair, making the bed, brushing teeth, washing hands, etc. Be sure to include the written description below the picture to encourage the word/picture correlation. Choose a child to look at the picture and pantomime the activity. The first child that guesses correctly gets the next turn.

"STAYING HEALTHY" BOOK. Using the ideas the children generated for the "Healthy Habits Chart", or the activities on the picture cards, put together a class book. On each page, place a photo of each child acting out a "staying healthy activity." Write a description of the activity of the page.

MULTI- CULTURAL

SING IN ANOTHER LANGUAGE. If you have any parents or children that speak another language, ask them to help you sing this song using some words in that language. For example, in French "hands" is *les mains*, and in Spanish, *los manos,* so you would sing:

This is the way we wash *les mains* ...(French)
This is the way we wash *los manos*...(Spanish)

RELATED ACTIVITIES

BABY DOLL WASHING. Set up a baby doll washing area with a baby bathtub, soap, wash cloths, towels and washable dolls. Try to have boy dolls as well as girl dolls and dolls representing various ethnic groups.

CLASSROOM VISITORS. Invite a doctor, nurse, dentist or dental hygienist to talk to the class about good health practices. You could also ask a P.E. teacher to talk about how exercise keeps them healthy and lead them in some fun activities.

BABY PICTURES. Ask parents to send in some of the children's old baby clothes and a baby picture of the child. Show the tiny clothing and discuss how eating healthy foods and following good practices has enabled them to grow from being babies to becoming children. Make a bulletin board showing baby pictures and current pictures of the children.

RELATED MUSIC

Brush Your Teeth
Oats, Peas, Beans
Rock Around the Mulberry Bush (by Greg and Steve)

RELATED LITERATURE

Ehlert, Lois. (1987). **GROWING VEGETABLE SOUP.** New York: Harcourt.

Dalton, Anne.(1992). **THIS IS THE WAY.** New York: Scholastic.

Henkes, Kevin. (1982). **CLEAN ENOUGH.** New York: Greenwillow.

MY AUNT CAME BACK

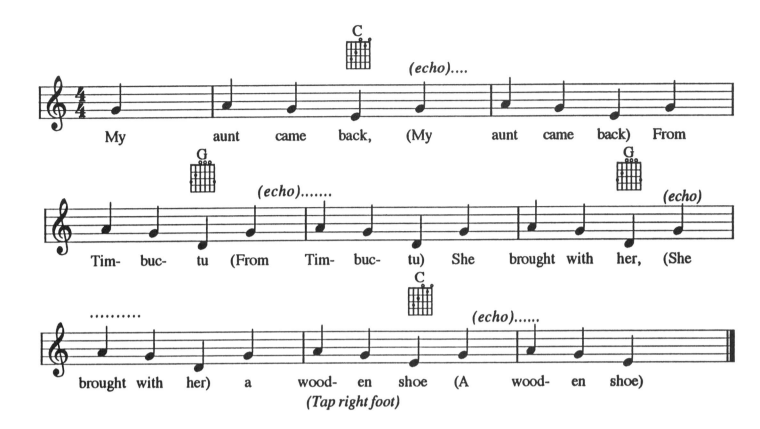

2. My aunt came back from old Algiers,
   She brought with her a pair of shears. (*pretend to cut with left hand*)

3. My aunt came back from old Japan
   She brought with her a paper fan. (*fan self with hand*)

4. My aunt came back from old Belgium
   She brought with her some bubblegum. (*pretend to chew*)

5. My aunt came back from the country fair
   She brought with her a rocking chair. (*rock back and forth*)

LARGE GROUP TIME

ADDING MOTIONS. The traditional way to sing this song is to continue each motion while you add the next so that your whole body is moving in different directions. If this is too difficult for your students just do one, two, or three verses.

ONE AT A TIME. Pick a different child to do each motion for the verses. Have them stand together and continue to do their motion while the next child adds his/hers. Three and four year olds can just stand up one at a time if it seems too confusing to do it with continuous motion.

MAKE UP VERSES. Name a city, state, country or place and use your rhyme bank or rhyme cards to make up new verses:

My aunt came back from Ohio,
She brought with her a big black crow (*flap arms*)

USE PROPS. Collect the items mentioned in the song and choose children to use them as the you sing the song.

CURRICULUM INTEGRATION

TRAVEL / VACATION
TRANSPORTATION
AROUND THE WORLD

SCIENCE

HOW COULD WE GET THERE? Show pictures of different forms of transportation. Point out on a globe or map where the class is located and where the aunt went. What type of transportation could you use to get to where she went?

LOOK AT MOTORS. Take children to the parking lot to look at the engine of your car. Arrange for the bus driver to arrive a little early and look and the engine of the bus. You probably could find a parent that is knowledgeable about engines to come in and talk to the children and even demonstrate how an engine works.

MOTOR OR NO MOTOR. Show an assortment of pictures of transportation modes such as cars, trucks, roller skates, horses, sailboat, ocean liner. Have the children tell you if it has a motor or no motor.

MATH

THINGS WITH WHEELS. Have the children either bring in or look around the room and collect things with wheels. Count how many wheels have been collected.

PLAY "WHAT'S MISSING?" The children are shown three to five items or feltboard cut outs of the items in the song. Hide the items with a screen or large paper and remove one item. Show the children what is left and they guess what's missing. For older children use more items and take away more than one item for them to guess what's missing.

SORT AND CLASSIFY. Provide an assortment of toy transportation items. Children can sort and classify them.

(ART)

PAPER AIRPLANES. Children of all ages love to fly paper airplanes. Children under 5 years old can decorate the paper with markers but will probably need an adult to fold the paper into planes. Children 5 and older may be able to follow a folding pattern. You can probably get some fifth and sixth graders to help the children fold the planes. Take the planes outside and see whose flies the furthest, the highest, the straightest, etc.

CUT AND GLUE. The children can look through magazines and cut and glue pictures of types of transportation. Remind them to look for things that use motors and things that do not use motors.

APPLIANCE BOX FUN . Obtain a large appliance box from a local appliance store. The children can decide if they would like to make it into a bus, a plane, a train, a boat, etc. They can paint the box and add details using construction paper, aluminum foil, and other materials.

(WHOLE LANGUAGE / READING)

HOW I SPENT MY VACATION. When children return after vacation, you can use this song to talk about and write about what they did. Use the child's name and where they went and make up a funny rhyme:

> When Matt came back from Disneyland,
> He brought with him a rubber band. (*pretend to stretch rubber band*)

"MY AUNT CAME BACK" BOOK. Using either the original verses or the new verses the children make up, create a class book. Children can illustrate the pages by either drawing or painting a picture of what the aunt brought back or by using magazine cut-outs.

RHYME BANK. Add to your rhyme bank things that rhyme with transportation modes such as boat, train, car, skate, bike, horse, etc.

(MULTI-CULTURAL)

IN DEPTH STUDY. Focus on one place that the aunt visited and do an in-depth study of that area: foods, customs, transportation, animals, houses.

WHAT ELSE WAS THERE? Choose one or two places that the aunt visited and research a typical or traditional food, type of house, clothing item, toy. Show photos or get the actual items. For example:
    France- French bread, a picture of a country house, a beret
    Mexico- Tortillas, a picture of a hacienda, a sombrero
    England- Scones, a picture of a castle, an umbrella
    Japan- White rice, a picture of a Japanese house, a Japanese fan or
        kimono.

RELATED ACTIVITIES

MOVE LIKE A HORSE. Put on some upbeat music. Name a mode of transportation and have the children move like they are using that type of transportation. They can pretend to ride a horse, row a boat, ride a bike, sit on a bus, ride on skateboard, etc.

FIELD TRIPS. Call your local airport, bus station or train station and arrange a field trip. Sometimes you can arrange for the children to sit in an airplane, bus, or train for 5-10 minutes while it's in the station or, in the case of an airplane, while its on the ground.

SET UP A TRAVEL AGENCY. Provide an area in the room to be a travel agency. Have pretend money, tickets, and travel brochures. Set up rows of chairs to simulate an airplane or bus or train. The children can plan their vacation and then pretend to travel there.

RELATED MUSIC

Moving Game (by Hap Palmer)
Wheels on the Bus
Row Row Row Your Boat
She'll Be Comin' 'Round the Mountain

RELATED LITERATURE

Burningham, John. (1972). **MR. GRUMPY'S MOTOR CAR.** New York: Thomas Y. Crowell.

Gibbons, Gail. (1983). **NEW ROAD! N.Y.:** Harper and Row.

Kovalski, M. (1987). **THE WHEELS ON THE BUS.** Boston: Little-Brown & Co.

Rockwell, Anne. (1986). **THINGS THAT GO**. New York: E.P. Dutton

Quackenbush, Robert. (1973). **SHE'LL BE COMIN' 'ROUND THE MOUNTAIN.** Philidelphia: Lippincott.

OH, WHEN THE SAINTS GO MARCHING

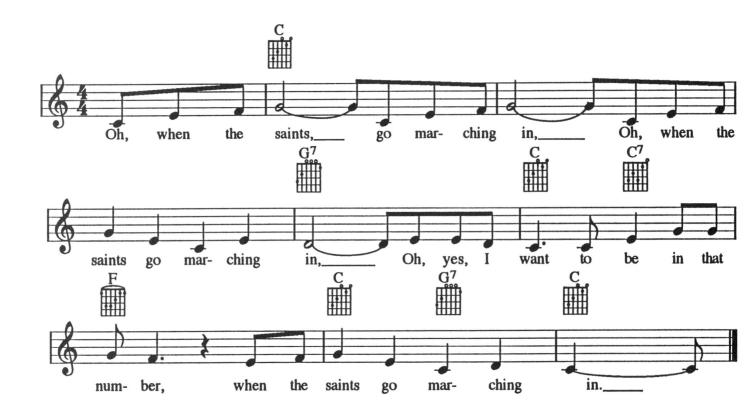

Oh, when the saints,____ go mar- ching in,____ Oh, when the
saints go mar- ching in,____ Oh, yes, I want to be in that
num- ber, when the saints go mar- ching in.____

(LARGE GROUP TIME)

PLAY INSTRUMENTS. Since this is a traditional marching song, let
the children march with your classroom instruments. First have them
practice playing in place, then play while marching.

FOLLOW THE LEADER. Play this game while marching either with
or without instruments. Change leaders often so that everyone gets a turn.

CHANGE THE WORDS. Divide the children into groups according to
which instrument they are playing. Instead of the words "Oh, when the
saints go marching in," sing, "When the class comes marching in," or,
"When the band comes marching in." All the children play instruments
together until you sing about their instruments individually, "Oh, when the
drums come marching in," at which time only the children playing that
instrument play and/ or march.

FOLLOW THE CONDUCTOR. Choose one child to be the conductor
of the band. He/She can direct the children to play their instruments louder
or softer, faster or slower.

CURRICULUM INTEGRATION

FIVE SENSES (SOUND)
PATRIOTIC HOLIDAYS

SCIENCE

MAKE INSTRUMENTS. Here a few ideas:

Shakers- Lay some paper plates on the table, put a handful of beans in the middle of each plate. Place another paper plate on top, curved side out. Either glue the plates or staple around the perimeter at frequent intervals. They shake them to make a sound.

Guitars- Have the children bring in a shoebox or tissue box. Stretch rubber bands over the opening. Children can strum or pluck the "strings."

Sand Blocks- Cut pieces of wood into pairs of 3 x 5 inch blocks. Glue or staple pieces of sandpaper on the bottom of each block. Children play them by rubbing the two blocks together.

Rhythm Sticks- Saw 1/4 or 1/2 inch wooden dowels into 10 inch lengths. Children can sand the ends until they are smooth. Play them by tapping two sticks together.

MATH

FLAG MATH. Count the number of stars and stripes on the American flag. You can also give the children a set of 50 star cut outs and have them separate them into groups of two's, fives, and tens.

SHAPE MARCHING. Place some large triangle, circle, and square shapes on the floor either with tape or by using paper shapes. Play marching music while the children march in a circle around the shapes. When the teacher stops the music, everyone gets inside a shape. Ask each group to call out the name of their shape before going on.

MARCHING 2 X 2. Let the children try marching in rows 2 x 2, 3 x 3, and in single file. Don't expect children under 6 years old to be able to stay in lines while they march, but they might enjoy trying.

ART

DECORATE INSTRUMENTS. Using paint and collage materials, decorate the instruments you made as described under the Science heading.

MUSICAL PAINTING. Play different types of music while the children paint with various objects such as brushes, feathers, feather dusters, kitchen implements, toothbrushes, etc. Vary the type of music you play and see if the different moods of waltzes, marches, folk, jazz or rock music change the way the children paint.

FLAGS. Make flags to carry while marching. Children can use red, white, and blue paper and/or paint and can copy the American flag or they can create their own original design. It is easy to copy the American flag by providing the children with white rectangles on which to glue precut red strips of construction paper, blue squares, and precut stars. When finished, tape or staple the flags to dowel sticks.

FIREWORKS. Dip "tuffy" sponges into tempera and print onto dark paper.

WHOLE LANGUAGE / READING

WORD CHART: Ask children what types of things they might see in a parade. Write their ideas on chart paper or on the chalkboard.

PARADE BOOKS. Create a class book similar to **PARADE** by Donald Crews. You can use the word chart you made in the above activity. Older children can draw or paint pictures to illustrate each page. Younger children can cut out pictures from magazines or coloring books.

MULTI-CULTURAL

FLAGS FROM AROUND THE WORLD. Bring in flags from around the world. Sometimes you can purchase miniature paper flags at party goods stores. Show on a globe or world map where the country from which each flag came is located.

INTERNATIONAL FESTIVAL. Invite families to bring in dolls, clothing, music, etc., from their ethnic background for an international festival. Ask each family to talk briefly about their contribution.

RELATED ACTIVITIES

BE IN A PARADE. If your school or local high school or community has a parade for homecoming, St. Patrick's Day or another holiday, see if you students can march along or ride on a float. If you walk in a parade, bring along some enthusiastic parents pulling wagons in which you can put tired children. If the children can't be in a parade, at least try to encourage parents to take the children to watch one.

RELATED MUSIC

Yankee Doodle
Grand Old Flag
America the Beautiful
Sousa Marches (instrumental)

RELATED LITERATURE

Crews, Donald.(1983). **PARADE.** New York: Greenwillow.

Joosse, Barbara. (1985). **FOURTH OF JULY**. New York: Knopf.

Keller, Holly. (1985). **HENRY'S FOURTH OF JULY.** New York: Greenwillow.

Wildsmith, Brian. (1982). **BEARS' ADVENTURE.** New York: Pantheon.

ONE ELEPHANT

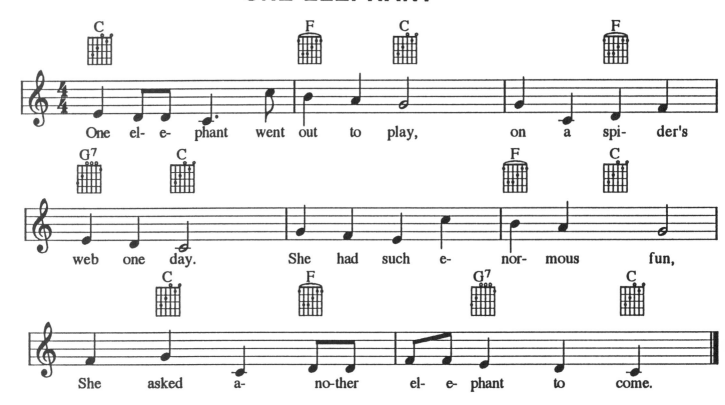

One el- e- phant went out to play, on a spi- der's web one day. She had such e- nor- mous fun, She asked a- no-ther el- e- phant to come.

2. Two elephants...   3. Three elephants...
Continue singing adding another elephant each time.

LARGE GROUP TIME

CIRCLE GAME. Children sit in a circle. One child is the elephant and walks around the outside of the circle. He/she taps another child to join in at the end of the song. Continue singing about the new number of elephants.

OTHER ANIMALS. Ask the children what other animals they would like to sing about walking along the spider web. Have the children pretend to walk like that animal. It's fun to use this song for your unit about dinosaurs:
    One dinosaur went out to play upon a spider web one day...

COPY THE ELEPHANT. Pick one child to be the elephant. The elephant chooses a motion for the other children to imitate while they sing. The elephant then chooses the next child to come to the center.

SPIDER WEB. You can design a large spider web on the floor with yarn and have the children walk along it as if on a tightrope.

ELEPHANT NECKLACES. Cut out elephants from different colors of paper. String a piece of yarn through the top in order to make a necklace for each child. Change the words of the song to represent the cut out elephant colors. The children join in the center of the circle when you sing about their color:

    A pink elephant went out to play on a spider's web one day...
    ...she asked for a blue elephant to come.

CURRICULUM INTEGRATION

ELEPHANTS
ZOO
SPIDERS
CIRCUS
DINOSAUR
FRIENDS

SCIENCE

OBSERVE A SPIDER. Catch a non-poisonous spider and observe it. Have the children draw pictures, dictate or write about their observations. If you prefer, you may be able to locate an active spider web in its natural environment to observe.

SPIDER WEB FUN FACT. Ask the children how they think the spider avoids getting stuck in her own web. Spiders make some strands sticky in order to catch their prey and leave other strands dry. The spider knows which is which and only steps on the dry strands.

WEB COLLECTION. Take the class on a spider web hunt. When you find an abandoned web, sprinkle talcum powder on it and carefully lift it by placing a black piece of construction paper behind the web and gently lifting the web with the paper.

MATH

COMPARE SIZES. Show pictures of different animals or insects and ask the children to tell you which is bigger, smaller, longer, shorter, etc.

COUNT ELEPHANTS ON A WEB. Provide each child with a sheet of paper on which you have drawn a spider web. Three and four year olds can paste or stamp elephant shapes on the web. Count how many elephants the child placed on the web and write the numeral on the page. Fives and older can have the numeral already written on the page and can stamp or glue the correct number elephants.

ELEPHANT NECKLACES. Put numerals on cut out elephant shapes strung on a necklace. Sing about each number and the child wearing that number goes into the circle:
> Number four elephant went out to play on a spider's web one day...
> ...he/she called for number 6 to come.

(ART)

YARN WEBS. The children can create "spider webs" by dipping pieces of yarn in either glue or liquid starch and laying a spider web design on wax paper. After it dries, the web can be lifted off and hung on a wall or from the ceiling.

WEAVE-A-WEB. Cut six slits around the perimeter of a paper plate. Children can weave a web by wrapping long strands of yarn around the plate into the slits.

WHAT COLOR IS AN ELEPHANT? Talk about the color of elephants. What else is gray? (sky, mouse, car) Demonstrate how to make gray by combining black and white tempera. The children can either paint with gray paint you've already prepared or can mix their own shades of gray using black and white fingerpaint or tempera paint.

(WHOLE LANGUAGE / READING)

WHERE ELSE COULD THE ELEPHANT PLAY? Children who are doing representational art (around 4 1/2 and older) can draw pictures and write new verses for where else the elephant could play, maybe in a pond, up a tree. Younger children cut out magazine pictures of someplace else where the elephant might play and glue precut elephants on the picture.

SILLY STORY. Ask the children if this song could ever happen. Tell them that they are going to write a class story about something as silly as this song. Give them a basic narrative and let them fill in the blanks to make a silly story. For example:

One bright morning when the moon was out, I saw a _____ walking down the street. It came up to me and said, "_____." Before I could answer, it disappeared behind a _____. Then...

MULTI-CULTURAL

ELEPHANTS AROUND THE WORLD. Other countries such as India and Africa use elephants as transportation and even use them for heavy labor. Go to the library and find some books that show elephants being used this way. Display the books in your reading or science area.

RELATED ACTIVITIES

BOOK DISPLAY. Display books about spiders and books about elephants.

FRIENDS. Talk about how the elephants were friends and wanted to play together. Ask the children what they should do in order to get someone to play with them. What do friends do to show they like each other?

RELATED MUSIC

There Was An Old Lady
Little Miss Muffet
Eentsy Weentsy Spider
Animal Fair
The Elephant (by Hap Palmer)

RELATED LITERATURE

Carle, Eric. (1984). **THE VERY BUSY SPIDER.** New York: Philomel.

de Brunhoff, Laurent. (1986). **BABAR'S COUNTING BOOK.** New York: Crowell.

MacDonald, Suse. (1991). **SPACE SPINNERS.** New York: Dial Books for Young Readers.

OVER IN THE MEADOW

O-ver in the mea-dow in the sand in the sun lived an old mo-ther tur- tle and her lit- tle tur- tle one. "Dig," said the mo- ther, "I dig," said the one, so they dug all day in the sand in the sun.

2...where the stream runs blue,
Lived an old mother fish
And her little fishies two.
"Swim" said the mother,
"We swim," said the two,
So they swam all day where
The stream runs blue.

3...in a hole in a tree,
Lived an old mother owl
And her littler owls three.
"Whoo-o," said the mother,
"We whoo-o," said the three,
So they "Whoo-o'd all day
In a hole in a tree.

4...near the old barn door,
Lived an old mother rat
And her little ratties four.
"Gnaw," said the mother,
"We gnaw," said the four,
So they gnawed all day
By the old barn door.

5... in a snug beehive
    bee... "Buzz"

6...nest full of sticks,
    crow..."caw"

7...where the grass grows even,
    frog..."jump"

8...near the old mossy gate,
    lizard..."bask"

9...near the old Scotch pine,
    duck..."quack"

10...in a cozy wee den,
    beaver..."beave

70

IN THE MEADOW. Ask the children if any one knows what a meadow is. If not, explain that it is like a field of grasses that may have trees or water nearby. Has anyone been in a meadow? What other animals might live there?

NEW VERSES. Make up new verses for other animals that live near the meadow:

> Over in the meadow in a hole in a tree,
> Lived an old mother squirrel
> And her little squirrels three.
> "Gather," said the mother,
> "We gather," said the three,
> So they gathered all day in a hole in a tree,

MAKE UP MOTIONS. As you sing each of the verses, have the children make up motions.

ACT IT OUT. Choose groups of children to act out the verses. This makes a cute parent program. Adding costumes makes it even better!

WHAT MAKES THIS SOUND? Use instruments for the animal sounds or find creative ways to make the sounds in the song. For example, they can scratch the carpet for "dig," a child can drop a toy into a basin of water for "swim."

FLANNELBOARD CUTOUTS. Prepare flannelboard cutouts of the animals and have the children put them up in order.

CURRICULUM INTEGRATION

HABITATS
ANIMALS
COUNTING
MOTHERS AND BABIES

SCIENCE

OBSERVE A HABITAT. Construct a terrarium and have the children collect insects or reptiles to put inside.

HABITAT SONG. When learning about habitats use this song to motivate children to think about what lives in which habitat. Change the words to fit each habitat:

Way down in the ocean where it's deep and blue,
Lived an old mother whale and her little calves two...

"ANIMAL-SITTING." Find someone to lend the class a turtle, fish, bird or another animal sung about in the song (or if you love owning pets, buy one for them!) For children three and four years old, the teacher can record the children's daily or weekly observations of the animals. Children older than four and a half can draw illustrations. First or second graders can write their own accounts of what they see.

VISIT A MEADOW. If you are fortunate enough to have a meadow near your school, visit it several times a year. Each time record the children's observations. They can take photograph, shoot videotapes, and draw pictures of what they see.

MEADOW COLLECTIONS. On a visit to the meadow, encourage the children to make collections of things they may find such as pieces of bark, rocks, dried flowers, leaves, fallen twigs, grasses. Remind them not to disturb any living things like flowers or insects. You could keep an ongoing display on the science table.

MATH

FINGER COUNTING. As simple as it sounds, have the children hold up the correct number of fingers as you sing. Children under five often have trouble putting up the correct number of fingers.

NUMBER CARDS. Prepare sets of number cards with either numerals, dots or animals representing number amounts, or both, depending on the level of your students. As you sing the song, the children hold up the card with the correct number represented.

MATCHING SETS. Create matching cards that go with the song and children can match them during small group or free time. The cards could consist of a matching set of a numeral 1 or one dot that will match to a picture of a turtle; a numeral 2 or 2 dots that will match with two fish.

MOTHERS AND BABIES. Show the children pictures of the mother animals in the song and ask them to match them to pictures of the baby animals.

ART

PUPPETS. Make puppets to represent the animals in the song. The puppets can be as simple as drawings supported by a craft stick. Other ways to make puppets include sock puppets and paper bag puppets. Use buttons, fabric, yarn, paper, ribbons, etc. for the features.

MEADOW COLLAGE. When the children make their collections on your trip to the meadow, have them pick out some items to use in a collage when they get back to the classroom. They can glue these items on heavy paper, foam trays or pieces of cardboard.

NATURE'S PAINTBRUSHES. Choose some items from a meadow such as grasses, pine cones, twigs, etc. Dip them in paint, brush across paper and create interesting textures with nature's paintbrushes.

WHOLE LANGUAGE / READING

ANIMAL CHARACTERISTICS. Show the children photos of animals such as those in the song, or plastic animals. Have the children describe various characteristics of each and record their responses on chart paper or the chalkboard. Examples might include:

hairy, webbed feet, tails, feathers, whiskers, hooves, claws

"IN THE MEADOW" BOOK. The children can write a book about what goes on in a meadow. If you visit a meadow, have them take along paper and marker or crayons with which they record what they see. If you are not able to visit a meadow, show pictures of and read books about the meadow and follow up with the children writing their own books.

MEADOW WORD CHART. Generate a word list of things in a meadow.

MULTI-CULTURAL

ANIMALS AROUND THE WORLD. In other cultures animals make different sounds than they do in English. For example a rooster that says "Cock-a-doodle-doo" in America says, "Ki-ka-ri-ki" in France, "Co-ca-ri-co," in Spanish and "Kikkehihi," in German. If you have families from different cultures in your program ask them to share these sounds in other languages with your class. You can also contact a local language center or college language department for this information.

MEADOWS AROUND THE WORLD. In different countries you will find different animals in their meadow. In England there are hedgehogs, in Australia kangaroos are commonly found.

(RELATED ACTIVITIES)

WHAT'S BEHIND THE WINDOW ? Take a large photo of an animal and cover it with a sheet of paper into which you have cut windows. Opening one window at a time reveals only a portion of the photo. See if the children can guess what animal it is without revealing the entire picture.

ANIMAL CRACKERS. Serve animal crackers for snacktime.

WHO AM I I? Give the children clues about an animal and have them guess which animal it is?
    I live in tree. I have a long bushy tail. I gather nuts. Who am I?

(RELATED MUSIC)

Six Little Ducks That I Once Knew
Five Little Ducks Went Swimming
Five Green and Speckled Frogs
There Was A Little Turtle

(RELATED LITERATURE)

Galdone, Paul. (1986). **OVER IN THE MEADOW: AN OLD NURSERY COUNTING RHYME.** New York: Clarion.

Pfloog, Jan. (1987). **WILD ANIMALS AND THEIR BABIES.** Racine, WI.:Western Publishing.

Scarry, Richard. (1976). **ABOUT ANIMALS.** Racine, WI.: Western Publishing.

Wadsworth, Olive A. (1986). **OVER IN THE MEADOW.** New York: Penguin Puffin.

Ziefert, Harriet. (1986). **SARAH'S QUESTIONS.** N.Y.: Lothrop, Lee and Shepard Books.

OVER THE RIVER

O- ver the riv- er and through the woods to grand- moth- er's house we go. The horse knows the way to car- ry the sleigh thru the white and drift- ed snow. O- ver the riv- er and through the woods, oh, how the wind does blow, it stings the nose and bites the toes as o- ver the ground we go.

LARGE GROUP TIME

DISCUSSION. To introduce this song, show a picture of a sleigh. Talk about how this was a common form of transportation before there were cars. Also, show a picture of a dapple gray horse so that they understand the song better.

KEEP THE RHYTHM. By tapping together two halves of a hollowed out coconut shell, you can make the sound of a horse trotting. Make the clip-clop sound first and have the children guess what makes that sound. Sing the song while making the sound of the horse clip-clopping through the snow. Give the children rhythm sticks , coconut shells and jingle bells to play while singing.

A MODERN THANKSGIVING SONG. Brainstorm how people now travel on Thanksgiving. Who do they visit, what do they eat for Thanksgiving dinner?
Incorporate their ideas into new verses:

> Over the highway or through the skies,
> To Grandmother's house we go;
> My dad knows the way, we'll get there today
> Even if it snows...
> Over the highways and through the skies,
> Now Grandmother's face I spy...

CURRICULUM INTEGRATION

THANKSGIVING
NATIVE AMERICAN CULTURE

SCIENCE

COOKING PROJECT. Bake a favorite Thanksgiving food like pumpkin pie, cranberry sauce, muffins, stuffing.

CORN. Discuss the important role the Native American Indians played in helping the Pilgrims learn how to grow crops. One of the most important and versatile crops was corn. Display a few varieties of corn and some products that are derived from corn such as: corn starch, corn flakes, popcorn, corn oil, corn meal, grits, dried corn, corn on the cob. You can even fill the sensory table with one of these items

A W, SHUCKS! Let the children shuck ears of corn. Point out the different part of the corn. Boil or steam the corn and serve for snack.

PUD. Add water to cornstarch to make a wonderful sensory mixture. It's messy but brushes off easily after it dries.

MATH

CORNY COUNTING. Cut the kernels off of a corn cob and let dry or buy dried corn. Count the kernels by ones, two's, fives, and tens. Have older children use the kernels as manipulatives for addition and subtraction.

BEAD MATH. Native Americans often traded beads for other items. Purchase beads at a craft store and have the children sort them before stringing necklaces. They can either copy a pattern or create their own design. They can also count the beads, compare who has more, less or the same amount. They can compare whose necklace is the longest and whose is the shortest.

TRADING POST. You could set up a store in which they use beads instead of money to barter for items. For children working with number recognition you could put price tags on items indicating how many beads each item costs.

IT'S A "MAZING." Create a maze on paper for children to trace the path to Grandmother's house. Increase the complexity according to the age of the children.

ART

A PICTURE PERFECT DINNER. Children can cut and glue magazine pictures of food that they would like to have for Thanksgiving dinner. They can glue the pictures to a paper plate.

FEATHER PAINTING. Purchase turkey feathers from a craft store for feather painting. The children can either dip the soft end in paint and sweep it across the paper, or you can make quill pens by cutting off the bare end at an angle. Dip the point in paint and write as if with a pen.

THANKSGIVING CENTERPIECES. Using a cup or bowl as a container, put some clay or playdough in the bottom and have the children stick dried flowers into it. You can either purchase dried flowers at a craft store or go into a field or meadow and pick your own assortment.

CORN COB PAINTING. Roll corn cobs in paint and then across paper. It makes an interesting design. Use corn holders to make it less messy!

77

CORNFLAKE TREES. Draw a simple tree trunk and branches. The children can glue cornflakes to the tree for a Fall picture.

WHOLE LANGUAGE / READING

WORD CHART. Brainstorm things about Thanksgiving. Write the words on chart paper or the chalkboard. You can also do a word chart about things for which we are thankful.

NATIVE AMERICAN PICTOGRAPHS. Show the children common Native American symbols and see if the children can guess what they represent. Write the English word underneath the Native American symbol. Children who are able to (usually over 4 1/2 years) might enjoy copying the symbols.

"TO GRANDMOTHERS HOUSE" BOOK. Using the modern day visiting song you wrote earlier (see Large Group Time), create a class book about going "over the highways and through the skies" to grandmothers house. Have the children draw pictures or use magazine cut outs for the illustrations.

MULTI-CULTURAL

NATIVE AMERICAN CULTURE. If you would like to include the Native American culture in your study of Thanksgiving, make sure not to stereotype. You might want to talk about how some people get the wrong idea from watching old T.V. westerns, but Native Americans hold jobs,wear blue jeans, go to school and buy food at the grocery store just like everyone else.. You can present facts about what life was for people in the 1500's , but be sure to discuss that things have changed in the Native American culture. Native Americans would prefer that schools do not dress children up in paper bag vests and construction paper headresses for their Thanksgiving celebration.

RELATED ACTIVITIES

VISITS AND VISITORS. Visit a local museum that has a Native American display. If that is not possible, invite a representative of the Native American community to discuss their heritage.

FAMILY FAVORITES THANKSGIVING DINNER. The class can cook part of the meal such as cornbread or pumpkin pie. Ask parents to bring their own family specialty. Before eating, have the children perform "Over the River" and any other Thanksgiving songs they may have learned.

GROCERY STORE. Set up a grocery store with empty cereal boxes, cans and pretend food for "shopping." Provide play money.

FRIENDSHIP SALAD. Each child brings in one piece of fruit to cut up and put into a salad. Invite parents or another class to come and share the harvest.

RELATED MUSIC

If You're Thankful and You Know It
He's a Big Fat Turkey On GrandFather's Farm
Did You Ever See A Turkey (Did You Ever See A Lassie Tune)

RELATED LITERATURE

Balian, Lorna. (1973). **SOMETIMES IT'S TURKEY, SOMETIMES IT'S FEATHERS.** Nashville: Abingdon Press.

Child, Lydia. (1992). **OVER THE RIVER AND THROUGH THE WOODS.** New York: Scholastic.

Gibbons, Gail. (1983). **THANKSGIVING.** New York: Holiday.

Nikola-Lisa, W. (1991). **1,2,3, THANKSGIVING.** Morton Grove, Ill: A. Whitman.

PEANUT BUTTER

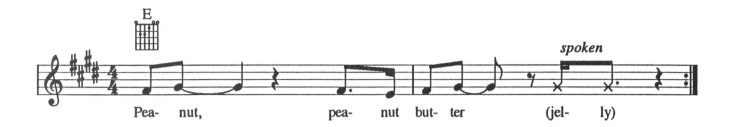

Pea- nut, pea- nut but- ter (jel- ly)

(spoken...)
1. First you take the peanuts and you dig 'em, you dig 'em, you dig 'em, dig 'em, dig 'em,
   Then you crush 'em, you crush 'em, you crush 'em, crush 'em, crush 'em,
   Then you spread 'em, you spread 'em, you spread 'em, spread 'em, spread 'em.
   (To Chorus)

2. Then you take the berries and you pick 'em, you pick 'em, you pick 'em, pick 'em,
   pick 'em,
   Then you smash 'em, you smash 'em, you smash 'em, smash 'em, smash 'em,
   Then you spread 'em, you spread 'em, you spread 'em, spread 'em, spread 'em.
   (To Chorus)

3. Then you take the sandwich and you bite it, you bite it, you bite it, bite it, bite it,
   And you munch it, you munch it, you munch it, munch it, munch it,(rub tummy)
   Then you swallow it, you swallow it, you swallow, swallow, swallow it,(make swallow
   noise)
   (To Chorus getting softer and softer)
   Make up motions to act out the words.

(LARGE GROUP TIME)

CLAP HANDS. Clap hands on "peanut butter". On "jelly," lean
forward, cup hands around mouth and whisper. Children five and older
might enjoy making up their own clapping patterns and motions.

OTHER FOODS. Ask the children what other foods you can sing about.
See if you can make up new verses. As you rewrite the verses, discuss how
the foods are obtained, processed or made. Other ideas could include:
   peanut butter and honey
   peanut butter and bananas
   pepperoni pizza (sing, "Pepper, pepperoni, pizza)
   macaroni and cheese (sing, "Mac, macaroni, and cheese)

(CURRICULUM INTEGRATION)

NUTRITION
FARMS
PEANUTS

SCIENCE

LOOK INSIDE A PEANUT. Split open a peanut and look at the baby plant waiting to grow on the inside on one of the nut halves.

PEANUT BUSH. These are available commercially through teacher supply catalogs or even in some toy stores. To grow one on your own you must use an unroasted nut.

NUTRITIONAL FACTS: Discuss the nutritional value of peanuts. Peanuts are part of a group called *legumes* and they contain lots of protein,

MAKE PEANUT BUTTER. With the shelled peanuts from the math activity make peanut butter. Put peanuts and a touch of peanut oil in a blender or food processor and grind until smooth. See the math activities for a way to make the shelling into a math activity.

SCIENCE TABLE. Place a variety of nuts and berries on the science table for the children to observe.

MATH

SHELL PEANUTS. Count how many peanuts each child has shelled. Arrange the peanuts in groups of two's, three's, fives, and tens.

COUNTING BY TWO'S. Most peanuts come two to a shell. Get a handful of peanuts in the shell and, counting by two's, predict how many peanuts you should have after they are shelled. Was your prediction correct? If not, does anyone remember opening a shell and finding one or three nuts in it?

FAVORITE PEANUT BUTTER GRAPH. Who prefers chunky peanut butter? Who likes smooth peanut butter best? Which brand to the children prefer? What is your favorite peanut butter sandwich? These are all questions whose responses work well to graph with the class? You might even want to have a taste session before the children put their responses on the graph.

THE PEANUT GAME. Use a spinner containing the numbers 1,2,3,4 or use dots instead of numbers depending on the age of your students. Each child spins and then takes that many number of peanuts.

PEANUT SHELL COLLAGE. Save the peanut shells you collect in the math activity and use them for a collage. You could cut pieces of construction paper in bread shapes and glue the shells on it.

FINGER PUPPETS. Draw faces on the top or bottom half of a shelled peanut shell. The children put the shell on their finger for a puppet.

PEANUT BUTTER AND JELLY PAINT. Cut paper in the shape of a slice of bread. Children can paint with light brown paint (the p.b.) and with purple paint (jelly.)

PEANUT BUTTER PLAYDOUGH. Combine a 16 oz. jar of peanut butter with a tablespoon of honey and enough powdered milk to make it a pliable consistency. The children will love to roll it , mold it and then eat their creations.

WHOLE LANGUAGE / READING

PEANUT BUTTER RECIPE. Before making peanut butter, ask the children to suggest ways to make it. Write their ideas on the board or on chart paper. After you've make the peanut butter, go back and look at the children's ideas. Have the children recall how you made it and rewrite the recipe. Make copies and send it home to parents.

PEANUT BUTTER AND JELLY BOOK. Take photographs of the children performing the motions of the song. Make a book with the photos and accompanying words on each page.

MULTI-CULTURAL

INTERNATIONAL FOOD FESTIVAL. P.B. and J is a favorite American food. Ask each family to look into their ethnic background and bring in a favorite food from that culture for your food festival. Invite parents and grandparents to the festivities. Show the children on a world map or globe the country from which the food originated.

RELATED ACTIVITIES

PICK BERRIES. If you live where berries grow, take a field trip to pick berries. If not, buy some berries at the store. Ask a parent to help you make jelly with the class.

PEANUT FEAST. Ask parents to send snacks made with peanuts for your peanut feast. Make sure that none of the students are allergic to peanuts. Here are a few ideas:

Celery stuffed with P.B.	P.B. and J. sandwiches
P.B. and honey sandwiches	P.B. and banana sandwiches
Peanut soup	Apples stuffed with P.B.

SENSORY TABLE. Add styrofoam "peanuts" to the sensory table.

RELATED MUSIC

Found a Peanut
A Peanut Sat on a Railroad Track
I Love Sandwiches
On Top of Spaghetti

RELATED LITERATURE

Banks, Kate. (1988). **ALPHABET SOUP.** New York: Knopf.

Barrett, Judi.(1982). Ill. by Ron Barrett. **CLOUDY WITH A CHANCE OF MEATBALLS.** New York: Atheneum.

Hoban, Russell, (1964). **BREAD AND JAM FOR FRANCES.** New York: Scholastic.

Illustrated by Nadine Westcott.(1987). **PEANUT BUTTER AND JELLY.** New York: Dutton.

RAIN SONGS

RAIN, RAIN GO AWAY

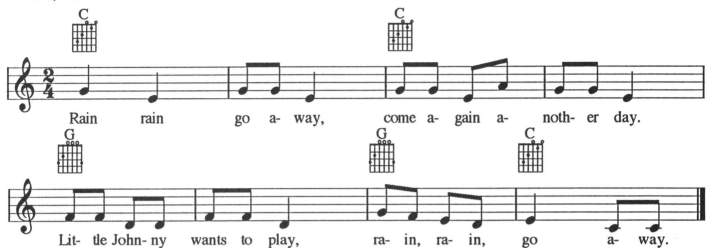

Rain rain go a- way, come a- gain a- noth- er day.
Lit- tle John- ny wants to play, ra- in, ra- in, go a- way.

IT'S RAINING, IT'S POURING

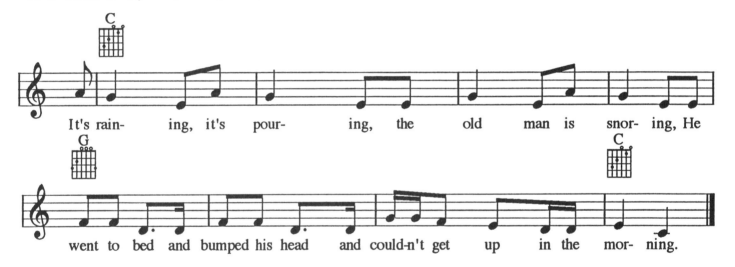

It's rain- ing, it's pour- ing, the old man is snor- ing, He
went to bed and bumped his head and could-n't get up in the mor- ning.

LARGE GROUP TIME

VARY THE VOLUME. Sing the song soft, medium, loud.

MAKE THE SOUND OF RAIN. How do the children think they can make the sound of the rain? They can tap fingers on the floor or on a table, tap pencils or rhythm sticks. Make the sounds while you sing . What words describe the sound of falling rain? (*Drip drop, splish splash, pitter patter.*) How could they reproduce the sound of thunder? Maybe they can rattle a baking sheet or stomp their feet.

THE OLD MAN IS SNORING. Choose a child or several children to act this out. One or several children can lay on the floor while they snore and bump their heads. Change "The old man is snoring" to the children's names:

> It's raining, it's pouring,
> Meagan and Alex are snoring...

CURRICULUM INTEGRATION

RAIN
WATER
WEATHER

SCIENCE

WATER AND PLANT GROWTH. Set up an experiment to demonstrate the importance of water for plant growth. Show the children two identical potted plants. What do plants need to survive? (*water, sun, oxygen*) What would happen if you didn't water one of the plants? Set up the plants side by side near a window. Every two or three days water one plant but not the other. Observe and record the changes that take place. The children can keep a diary by drawing pictures of the plants. After the one plant has dried up, have the children hypothesize what happened.

EVAPORATION. Give each child a clear plastic glass. Fill each glass 1/3 full and mark the water level and the date with a permanent marker. Every three to four days, look at the water and record the new level and the date. Where do the children think the water has gone? Explain how evaporation is an important cycle of nature.

MATH

PLANT SEEDS. Using small cups or egg cartons and planting soil, have the children plant seeds. Let them measure the growth by placing a craft stick in the soil and marking the height of the new growth with a pen. Have the children note whose plant is the tallest, shortest, whose has leaves first, whose blooms first and last.

WEATHER CALENDAR. Use symbols to represent clouds, sunshine, rain, and snow. Each day ask the students to choose the appropriate symbol for that day's weather. At the end of the week or after a month, count how many days of each type of weather there were.

RAIN GAUGE. Purchase or make a rain gauge out of a clear plastic cup with 1/4 inch markings you have drawn with permanent marker. Keep it in one place outside and check it after each rainfall. Keep a chart of the results and the dates.

UMBRELLAS. Ask children to bring in umbrellas from home. Make a graph of the different colors or patterns.

(ART)

RAINDROP PAINTING. Children can apply powdered tempera to paper with a cotton ball. They then spray the paper with water in a spray bottle and watch the colors run. If it's raining outside, they can just carry the paper outside with the powdered tempera and let the raindrops dampen it.

UMBRELLA PICTURES. Cut out umbrella shapes from a wallpaper or construction paper. The children can decorate them with paints or collage materials. These make a nice springtime bulletin board.

RAINBOW ART. The children draw on coffee filters with non-permanent markers. They then spray the filters with water in a spray bottle and watch the colors run into each other. They can also use stencils to trace umbrellas, raindrops, clouds and suns on paper towel (the cheaper, the better.) Spray with water bottles and watch the colors run.

(WHOLE LANGUAGE / READING)

RAIN POEM OR STORY. Write either a poem or a story about the rain with the class. It can be about what gets wet when it rains, why we like the rain, or why the rain is important. You could call it "The Best Thing About Rain."

(RELATED ACTIVITIES)

RAIN DAY. It doesn't have to rain to have a rain day at school. Tell the children to bring umbrellas, rain boots and raincoats for rain day. Arrange to set up a sprinkler and let the children have fun in the "rain." If it's warm out, they can just wear swimsuits.

RELATED MUSIC

If All the Raindrops Were Lemon Drops
Ducks Like Rain (by Franciscus Henri)
It Ain't Gonna Rain No More, No More

RELATED LITERATURE

Branley, Frankley M.(1985). Ill. by Barbara amd Ed Emberly. **FLASH, CRASH, RUMBLE, ROLL.** New York: Harper.

Ginsburg, Mirra. (1964). **MUSHROOM IN THE RAIN.** New York: MacMillan.

Scheer, Julan. (1964). **RAIN MAKES APPLESAUCE.** New York: Holiday House.

Speirs, Peter. (1977). **PETER SPEIR'S RAIN.** New York: Doubleday.

Yashima, Taro. (1977). **UMBRELLA.** New York: Penguin.

Stevenson, James. (1988). **WE HATE RAIN.** New York: Greenwillow.

Zolotow, Charlotte. (1952). **THE STORM BOOK.** New York: Harper and Row.

SKINNAMARINK

MAKE UP MOTIONS. Instead of using the traditional motions, have the class make up new motions.

AMERICAN SIGN LANGUAGE. You can say, "I love you" in ASL by pointing to yourself with your pointer (instead of pointing to your eye) and using the other motions in that part of the song. Learn the remainder of the song in American Sign Language and teach it to the class.. Ask as special education teacher or call your local Center on Deafness to help you.

SING IN GROUPS. Divide the children into two groups and have them alternate singing each line.

CURRICULUM INTEGRATION

VALENTINE'S DAY
MOTHERS DAY
FRIENDS

SCIENCE

FEEL THE BEAT. Talk about the human heart and how it pumps blood throughout the body. Have the children locate their own heart. Get a stethoscope and let the children listen to their heart through the stethoscope.

FAST AND SLOW HEARTBEAT. The children put their hand on their heart to feel it beat while at rest. Put on some upbeat dancing music and tell them to dance, jump or run in place until the music stops. As soon as you stop the music, the children once again place their hand on their heart and feel their accelerated heartbeat.

HEART-SHAPED GELATIN. Follow the directions on a box of red gelatin for "finger jello" or "wiggle shapes". When it has set, the children can cut out heart shapes with heart cookie cutters.

MATH

HEART MATCHING. Provide heart cut-outs in different sizes and colors for matching, seriation (putting in order from smallest to largest), and size comparison.

HEART CARDS. Using the heart cards from two decks of cards, the children can match cards. They also can take a card and then use the number of blocks indicated on the card to build a block tower. They can either build their own tower or build one tall tower together.

CARDS AND ENVELOPES. Provide a selection of different size valentine cards and envelopes. Children match the card to the envelope according to size. They can check their answer by putting the card inside the envelope.

HEART FISHING. Cut out heart shapes and write numerals, dots, shapes, or animals on matching pairs. Place a paper clip on each heart. Children use a dowel onto which you have attached a string with a magnet at the end in order to fish for matching hearts.

(ART)

HEART CUT-OUTS. Demonstrate how to draw and cut out a heart shape on a folded sheet of paper. Provide the children with scissors and some folded sheets on which you have already drawn a half heart. They cut through both sheets and then unfold it to reveal a whole heart. Children who are 5 and older can probably draw the half heart shape themselves.

DECORATE HEARTS. Children can decorate heart shapes with ribbons, lace, glitter, buttons or other collage materials for Valentine's Day cards or decorations.

STRING PAINTING. After children cut out their folded heart shapes they can take a string dipped in paint, place it in between the two halves while they are still folded and pull it through , leaving a path of paint on the inside. Open the heart to reveal the design made by the string.

(WHOLE LANGUAGE / READING)

I LIKE YOU BECAUSE. On chart paper or the chalkboard make a chart to fill in with each child's name:

    I like Mary because_____

    I like Josh because_____

Each day talk about a few children and why the other children like him/her. Write it on the chart for everyone to see.

I LIKE YOU" CATERPILLAR. Write positive comments about each child on heart shapes and attach them to form a long caterpillar along the wall.

"I LIKE YOU" BOOK. Make a book out of the "I like you because" chart. Place a photo of a child on each page and write the reason the other children like him/her. Keep it on the bookshelf or send it home with a different child each week so that the parents can read it to the child.

WHAT MAKES A FRIEND? Talk about which behaviors make someone want to be your friend. Write the responses on chart paper or on the board. Children can dramatize the correct way and incorrect way to act in different situations in order to make a friend:

*Your friend has a toy you'd like to play with.
*Someone in the class has built a very tall block tower and you're
    upset that you're having trouble building yours as tall.
*You're playing with your friend Angela. Derek wants to play with
    both of you, but Angela won't let him.

MULTI-CULTURAL

I LOVE YOU AROUND THE WORLD. Teach the children to say "I love you" in different languages:

French- *Je t'aime*   Spanish- *Te amo*

RELATED ACTIVITIES

PARENT PERFORMANCE. This a great song for a parent performance. On the words, "I love you," the children point to their parents in the audience.

FEELING SPECIAL. Each time you sing this with the children point to a different student when you sing the words, "I love you." It makes them feel special.

VALENTINE'S DAY VISIT. Take handmade valentines and cookies to a retirement home or apartment. Put on a brief program of songs or a play and end the performance by singing this song to the residents.

RELATED MUSIC

A Tisket, A Tasket
Mail Myself To You (by Woody Guthrie)
A Bicycle Built For Two

RELATED LITERATURE

Anglund, Joan Walsh.(1958). **A FRIEND IS SOMEONE WHO LIKES YOU.** New York: Harcourt, Brace and Jovanovich.

Carle, Eric. (1971). **DO YOU WANT A FRIEND?** New York: Putnam.

Devlin, Wende and Harry.(1988). **CRANBERRY VALENTINE.** New York: Macmillan.

Munsch, Robert. (1986). **LOVE YOU FOREVER.** New York: Firefly.

Silverstein, Shel. (1964). **THE GIVING TREE.** New York: Harper and Row.

TEN IN THE BED

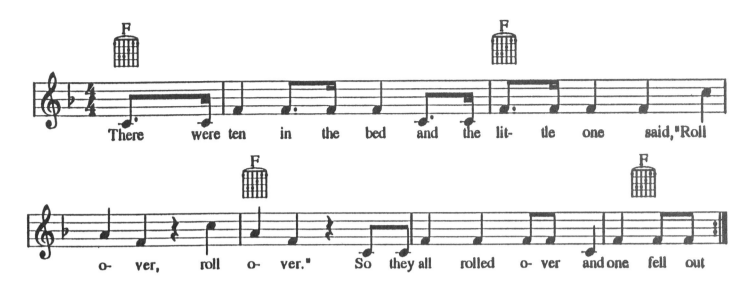

There were ten in the bed and the lit- tle one said, "Roll

o- ver, roll o- ver." So they all rolled o- ver and one fell out

Sing the other verses in descending numerical order. When you get down to one in the bed, she says "Good Night!"

(LARGE GROUP TIME)

ACT IT OUT. Children love to dramatize this song. Have ten children lay down on the floor pretending that they are in a bed. On "one fell out" they all roll over once in the same direction and the child on the end leaves the "bed." If you don't have the time or patience to do ten in the bed, just sing about five in the bed.

ANOTHER ENDING. What might the last child say other than, "Good Night?" Ask the children for other ideas. She might say, "I'm lonely," in which case you can start singing the song again adding one to the bed each verse by singing:

     ... so the *one* moved over and *one* got in,
     There were two in the bed and the little on said...

Or, to the tune of "He's Got the Whole World" sing, "I've got the whole bed to myself."

USE A CHILD'S NAME. Sing a child's name in place of "the little one" and that child can sing, "Roll over." "

FAST OR SLOW. Vary the tempo as you sing. The children's actions should reflect the tempo.

93

CURRICULUM INTEGRATION

COUNTING
NIGHT
BEDS / BEDTIME

SCIENCE

ANIMALS ASLEEP. Discuss how and where animals sleep. Are there any animals that sleep in a bed? Which animals sleep at night and are awake during the day? Do any of the children's moms or dads work at night and sleep during the day.

BED TEXTURES. A bed has many different textures from the hardness of the frame to the softness of the pillows. On your science table, put out various textures representative of the different parts of a bed. See if the children can figure out which part of the bed the textures feel most like.

MATH

BEANS IN A BED. Each child can have a small paper rectangle for a bed and 10 beans. As you sing each verse, they make one fall out and put it in a cup. Have them tell you how many are left before singing the next verse. You can also start with one in the bed and add beans one, two or three at a time. Change the words accordingly.

COMPARING BED SIZES. Find different sizes of doll or stuffed animal beds or make different sized beds out of boxes. Have some dolls or stuffed animals available and ask the children to predict which dolls will fit which bed. Try out their predictions.

MATCHING BEDS. There are several ways to do this activity. You can make sets of beds with matching bedspreads out of paper or index cards and have the children match them. Another way would be to make 10 beds out of library pockets with the numeral 1-10 on the outside. Create corresponding cards with 1-10 happy or sleeping faces on them and have the children match the cards to the pockets.

ART

BED COLLAGE. Create a texture collage on a bed shaped paper using soft, and hard items.

94

DOLL OR ANIMAL BLANKETS. Cut fabric in doll-size rectangles with pinking shears. Let them decorate it with fabric crayons or fabric paints. If you have a parent that sews, you might be lucky enough to get someone to sew some nice soft blankets for the children to decorate.

WHOLE LANGUAGE / READING

WORD CHART. Ask the children what they think it would feel like to sleep in a bed with nine other people. Write their responses on a word chart. Words might include *crowded, squished, fun, uncomfortable.*

WEEKLY BEDTIME STORY. Once a week pick a child to bring in their favorite bedtime story to be read to the class. It would be really special to arrange for that child's parent or grandparent to read the book to the class.

MULTI-CULTURAL

LULLABIES AROUND THE WORLD. Teach the children a lullaby from another country. If you do not know any, ask the parents and grandparents in your class if they know any they could teach the children. The French lullaby "Fais Dodo" is on a few children's music albums.

RELATED ACTIVITIES

BEDTIME STORY HOUR. Invite families to come to school one evening for a bedtime story hour. Your local library may be able to send a professional storyteller for a reasonable fee. The children can come in their pajamas and bring their blankets and pillows. Serve a bedtime snack of milk and cookies.

PILLOW DAY. Have children bring their favorite pillow to school on Pillow Day. Make a pillow pile for them to jump into.

HOUSEKEEPING AREA. Set up a doll bed with ten dolls or stuffed animals with which children can dramatize this song. You can make ten small dolls by wrapping clothespins with fabric and drawing faces on them.

BED BUGS GAME. You can purchase this game at most toy stores.

RELATED MUSIC

Lullabies:
Twinkle Twinkle
Hush Little Baby
Rock-a-by Baby
Fais Dodo (sung by Raffi)

Counting Songs:
Over in the Meadow
One Elephant

RELATED LITERATURE

Arnold, Ted. (1987). **NO JUMPING ON THE BED!** New York: Dial Books for Young Readers.

Koide, Tan.(1983). Illustrated by Yasuko Koide. **MAY WE SLEEP HERE TONIGHT?** New York: Atheneum Press.

Mayer, Mercer. (1987). **THERE'S AN ALLIGATOR UNDER MY BED.** New York: Dial Books for Young Readers.

Peek,Merle.(1981). **ROLLOVER! A COUNTING BOOK.** New York: Clarion Books.

Rees, Mary. (1988). **TEN IN THE BED**. San Francisco, Harper.

Wood, Audrey. (1984). Ill. by Don Wood. **THE NAPPING HOUSE.** N.Y.: Harcourt, Brace, and Jovanovich.

THE ANTS GO MARCHING

2. Two by two... tie his shoe
3. Three by three... climb a tree
4. Four by four... shut the door
5. Five by five... to take a dive
6. Six by six...pick up sticks

7. Seven by seven... look to heaven
8. Eight by eight... shut the gate
9. Nine by nine... spend a dime
10. Ten by ten... shout, "The End"

ACT IT OUT. This is a fun song to dramatize. The children can act out the motions in groups the size called for in the song or they can act out the motions in one large group.

NEW VERSES. Use your *rhyme bank* or use rhyme cards to make up new verses. This is a cute song to present at a parent meeting or for other classes.

MARCH LIKE OTHER ANIMALS. What do the children think an ant sounds like when it marches? How about an elephant or a tiger or a cat? Change the words to different animals and the children can march as if they were that animal. Have the children think of where each animal would go to "get out of the rain" and substitute those words for "down to the ground:"

> The bees went buzzing two by two...
>
> ...they all went marching back to the hive...

CURRICULUM INTEGRATION

ANTS
INSECTS
COUNTING

SCIENCE

ANT FARM. You can purchase commercially prepared ant farms from a variety of toy stores and teacher supply catalogs. If you prefer to make one yourself, you can use a plastic shoe box or glass jar. Punch small air holes in the lid and cover the holes with cotton balls so that the air can get in but the ants can't get out. Fill the container with dirt or sand. Go outside and find an anthill. Transfer some of the ants to the jar (they must be from the same anthill or they will kill each other.) For the first two days cover the container with a cloth, the darkness will encourage their tunneling. Be sure to feed the ants a few breadcrumbs and some drops of water every few days.

OBSERVE AN ANTHILL. Go outside with the children and find an anthill. Observe the ants and record the children's observations. Return periodically and compare the activity.

ANTS IN A BUG BOX. Place some ants in a bug box and observe their behavior. Have some paper and markers available nearby with which the children can draw pictures of the ants. At the end of the day return the ants to their anthill or wherever you found them.

ANT BOOKS. There are many different types of ants. There are carpenter ants, red ants and army ants to name a few. Obtain books on ants from the library and place them on or near the science area.

MATH

MARCH TWO BY TWO. Demonstrate either with children or by using plastic ants what it means to march two by two, three by three, etc. You can purchase bags of plastic ants to use as counters around Halloween.

SIX LEGS. Count how many legs an ant has. Ask the children to place pennies, marbles, buttons, etc. into groups of six. Ask them to bring in six like edible items from home. They could bring six grapes, six Cheerios, six raisins. Place the assortment of items out for snacktime and each child can choose six things to eat.

ARE YOU AS STRONG AS AN ANT? Ants can pick up and carry things that weigh up to fifty times their own weight. Put out items of various weights and let the children experiment to see what is the heaviest item they can pick up.

PLASTIC ANT COUNTERS. Make anthills or ant nests out of cups, egg cartons or muffin cups. Number them 1-6. Using plastic toy ants or raisins representing black ants, place the appropriate number of ants in each nest.

ART

BUILD AN ANT. For the head, thorax and abdomen use 3 styrofoam balls or marshmallows connected by short pieces of toothpicks. The six legs can be made of pipecleaners, toothpicks or even licorice laces.

ANTS IN THE ANTHILL. Draw a large anthill complete with tunnels on brown butcher paper. The children can put ants in the tunnels by pressing a finger into a stamp pad and then on the paper for fingerprint ants, or by stamping three dots with the end of a pencil eraser for the body parts and adding 6 legs with a marker.

WHOLE LANGUAGE / READING

ANTS IN YOUR PANTS. Talk about the meaning of funny expressions that use animals or insects such as "ants in your pants," for someone who is wiggly or impatient, "a bee in your bonnet" means someone is angry, "birdbrain" refers to someone who isn't very smart.

IF I WERE AN ANT. Ask the children to think of how it would feel to be the size of an ant. Write a class book "If I Were An Ant" and have the children illustrate it.

ANTS IN THE PANTS GAME. This game which is played like Tiddly Winks can be purchased at most toy stores.

RELATED MUSIC

Shoo Fly
Eentsy Weentsy Spider
Baby Bumblebee

other counting songs:
Ten in the Bed
One Elephant Went Out to Play
Over in the Meadow

RELATED LITERATURE

Cameron, Polly. (1961). **"I CAN'T," SAID THE ANT**. New York: Scholastic Book Services

Dorros, Arthur. (1987). **ANT CITIES**. New York: Harper and Row.

Myrick, Mildred. (1968). **ANTS ARE FUN.** New York: Harper and Row.

Van Allsburg, Chris. (1988). **TWO BAD ANTS.** Boston, Ma.: Houghton Mifflin.

THERE'S A HOLE IN THE BUCKET

There's a hole in the buck-et, dear Li-za, dear Li-za. There's a hole in the buck-et, dear Li-za, a hole. Well,___ fix it dear Hen-ry, dear Hen-ry, dear Hen-ry. Well, fix it dear Hen-ry, dear Hen-ry fix it.

2. With what shall I fix it, dear Liza, dear Liza?
   With what shall I fix it, dear Liza with what?
   With a straw, dear Henry, dear Henry, dear Henry,
   With a straw, dear Henry, dear Henry with a straw.

3. But the straw is too long...
   Well, then cut it...

4. With what shall I cut it?..
   With a knife...

5. The knife is too dull...
   Then sharpen it...

6. With what will I sharpen it?...
   With a stone...

7. But the stone it too dry...
   Well, wet it...

8. With what shall I wet it?...
   With water...

9. In what shall I carry it?
   In a bucket...

10. But, there's a hole in the
    bucket...
    Then fix it, dear Henry.

SING IN TWO PARTS. One child can be Liza and another can be Henry. You can use the children's names instead of "Liza" and "Henry." You can also split the class into two groups with one group singing the part of Liza and the other group singing the part of Henry.

DRAMATIZE. The children can pantomime cutting the straw, chopping with an axe, sharpening the axe.

REWRITE THE WORDS. Instead of singing the traditional words, let the children decide where to take the songs and rewrite the verses:

> With what shall I fix it?...
> With some tape...
> I can't find the tape...
> Well, buy some...

CURRICULUM INTEGRATION

HOLES
BUCKETS
COMMUNITY HELPERS

SCIENCE

BALANCING ACT. The children can experiment with a balance. You can purchase an elementary or preschool balance from teacher supply catalog. If you'd like to make your own, take a hanger and suspend a cup from a string at either end. Hang it from a hook or a doorknob.

BUCKETS OF FUN. Fill buckets with different amounts and weights of things. Children can carry a bucket of wooden blocks, a bucket of styrofoam packing peanuts, a bucket of water or sand. Which is heaviest, which is lightest, which is easiest to carry? Which is the hardest to carry?

HOLES IN THE BUCKETS. At the water table, provide buckets and containers with holes in them. Let the children come up with ideas on how to fix the holes. If possible, let them try out their ideas and see if they can fix the holes.

MATH

COUNT THE ITEMS. Count how many different items they use to try to fix the bucket. Either collect the items and count them, or make flannelboard pictures and count them.

FILL THE BUCKETS. Using buckets of different sizes, count how many cups or pitchers it takes to fill each one.

STRAWS AND SCISSORS. Give the children straws and scissors. They can cut the straws into different lengths. Compare the different sizes. Children can sort them into groups according to lengths. They can then make either a straw collage or string the pieces onto yarn to make a necklace.

NUMBER BUCKETS. Make small "buckets" by attaching a pipecleaner to the edge of a paper cup. Write a numeral on each cup. Give each child a handful of straw pieces. They put the correct number of straw pieces in each "bucket." For younger children who are not yet working with numbers, use colors or shape pictures on each "bucket" and the children can match the same picture on a small card to the picture on the "bucket."

WILL IT FIT? Give the children various size buckets. Have them find something that will fit inside. Next, have them find something that will not fit inside.

ART

"HOLEY" ART. Cut a hole in a piece of construction paper. The hole can be circular, square, oblong or an irregular shape. The children can paint or draw around the hole in the paper.

STRAW BLOWING PAINTING. Drop 2 or 3 spoonfuls of thin tempera on construction paper. Give each child a straw with which to blow on the paint and spread it over the paper.

OUTSIDE PAINTING. If weather permits, take buckets of water and paintbrushes outside for the children to paint the fence, walls and playground equipment. You can color the water with food coloring if you'd like.

STRAW SCULPTURES. Children can stick straws into playdough for straw sculptures.

WHOLE LANGUAGE / READING

"HOLE IN THE BUCKET" BOOK. Use the new verses the class wrote for the song to create a class book. Write each verse on each page. The children can either draw pictures, use magazine cut-outs, or glue some of the actual items onto the page for illustrations. On the page "With what shall I..." you can just write a large question mark: ???

WORD CHART. Why do we use buckets? How many different uses for buckets can the children think of? Write their responses on chart paper or on the board.

RELATED ACTIVITIES

HOLES FROM HOME. Ask the children to bring something from home that has a hole or holes in it. Examples might include: a fly swatter, an angel food cake pan, a bagel, buttons, straws, hoop earrings, a hula hoop.

COMMUNITY HELPERS. Which community helpers might use a bucket? (custodians, farmers, painters)

RELATED MUSIC

Other call and response songs:
Muffin Man
Feed My Cow
Pussy Cat, Pussy Cat

RELATED LITERATURE

Barton, Byron. (1981). **BUILDING A HOUSE.** New York: Greenwillow.

Florian, Douglas, (1983). **PEOPLE WORKING.** New York: Harper.

Krauss, Ruth. (1952). **A HOLE IS TO DIG.** New York: Harper.

Stubbs, William. (1983). **THERE'S A HOLE IN MY BUCKET.** Oxford.

THIS OLD MAN

This old man, he played one, he played nick- nack on my thumb, with a nick- nack pad- dy- whack give the dog a bone, This old man came rol- ling home.

2. Two... shoe
3. Three... knee
4. Four... door
5. Five... hive

6. Six... sticks
7. Seven... up to heaven
8. Eight... gate
9. Nine... spine
10. Ten... once again

LARGE GROUP TIME

PLAY KNICK-KNACK?   What does it mean to "play knick-knack?"
Ask the children to show their own version of "playing knick-knack"
during that part of the song.

PLAY INSTRUMENTS. Think of an instrument sound for "knick-
knack paddy-whack." On those words, children play their instrument.
What else can the Old Man do other than "play knick-knack?" Maybe he
can clap or laugh:

> This Old Man, he can laugh,
> He can laugh at that giraffe...
> This Old Man, he can clap,
> He can clap and tap, tap, tap...

USE A CHILD'S NAME. Use the children's names instead of "This
Old Man" and that child can decide which rhyme to use and how to act it
out:

> Joshua, he played one; He played one on a big, big drum...

105

MAKE UP MOTIONS. Most children are already familiar with the motions for this popular song. Hold up the appropriate number of fingers when that number is sung, for "knick knack"criss cross your pointer fingers, pantomime the activity. For "knick- knack paddy-whack give the dog a bone" pat your knees twice, then clap your hands twice. On "rolling home" roll hands over one another in circular motion.

CURRICULUM INTEGRATION

COUNTING
GRANDPARENTS
PETS
SHOES
BONES

SCIENCE

BONE COLLECTION. Collect a variety of bones and place them on the science table. You can easily save chicken, turkey and beef bones by asking parents to bring in clean, boiled bones. Ask your local butcher for some donations.

BAKE COOKIES. Since many children do not live near their grandparents and get little exposure to senior citizens, invite grandparents or other Senior Citizens in for tea, class-baked cookies, and a performance.

MATH

NUMBER CARDS. Each child can be given either one number card or a set of number cards depending on the age and abilities of the children. As they sing the song, the children hold up the appropriate cards. The cards could have either a numeral, dots representing the number, or both.

FROM 10 TO 1. Sing the song in descending order from 10 to 1. Have the numbers written on the board or chart, or use flannelboard numbers in order to help the children see which number comes next.

SORTING BONES. Taking the bones you have collected for the science table, have the children sort and classify them according to size, shape, length, weight. You could also use dog biscuits. They come in assorted colors and sizes.

GROUPS OF TEN. Ask the children to bring from home 10 of one item. Put them out in groups of ten and demonstrate how to count by tens.

NUMBER BOOK. Number pages 1-10. Children glue the correct number of items on each page. They can glue beans, pieces of paper, or try to find pictures of things that go with the song for each page.

ART

THUMBPRINT PICTURES. Spread thick tempera onto a sponge. Children press their thumb onto the sponge then onto a piece of paper. When it has dried, the children can add faces, legs, hats etc. with markers or crayons.

GRANDMA AND GRANDPA CUT OUTS. Have the children look through magazines and cut out pictures of people who might be grandmothers and grandfathers. They can glue the pictures on construction paper.

WHOLE LANGUAGE / READING

"THIS OLD MAN" BOOK. Ask the children how they think they could represent each of the verses. For example:
>   a shoe print or magazine picture of a shoe for "2"
>   a magazine picture of a knee for "3"
>   a hinged door cut out of constructions paper for "4"
Each child can choose which number he/she wants to work on.

NEW VERSES. Children who are able to rhyme can help to write new verses. If the children are unable to rhyme, give them some choices of good rhymes to use. Write the new verses in a class book and have the children either decorate or illustrate the pages. Send the book home with a different child each weekend and have a few blank pages at the end for parents' comments.

MULTI-CULTURAL

COUNTING IN DIFFERENT LANGUAGES. Teach the children to count in a foreign language. If there are any bilingual or foreign speaking students in your class, have them teach the other students. Depending on the age and abilities of your students, they can learn to count to three, five, ten or higher in a foreign language with great success.

RELATED ACTIVITIES

THIS OLD MAN?   Ask the children who they think "this old man" could be. Talk about the term "old man" not being a very nice way to refer to older people. Who do they know that is "old." Most likely, you will have a lively discussion about grandparents. What kinds of things can the children think of to do to help older people with whom they might spend time?

PERFORM FOR SENIOR CITIZENS. Prepare some songs, dances or plays to perform for senior citizens. It may be scary for young children to visit a retirement home where seniors are extremely ill, so you may want to visit a site yourself before going with children. Also, there are many senior citizen groups with active, lively seniors who would welcome a visit from your youngsters.

RELATED MUSIC

There Was An Old Lady
Grandma's Spectacles
This Old Man (jazzy version by Greg and Steve)
other counting songs

RELATED LITERATURE

DePaola, Tomi. (1973). **NANA UPSTAIRS, NANA DOWNSTAIRS.** New York: Putnam.

Koontz, Robin. (1988). **THIS OLD MAN: THE COUNTING SONG.** Dodd Mead.

Mayer, Mercer. (1985). **JUST GRANDPA AND ME.** New York: A Golden Book.

Mayer, Mercer. (1985). **JUST GRANDMA AND ME.** New York: A Golden Book.

Row, Eileen. (1989). **STAYING WITH GRANDMA.** New York: Bradbury.

Scarry, Richard. (1975). **THE BEST COUNTING BOOK EVER.** New York: Random.

THREE BEARS CHANT

Once upon a time in a nursery rhyme
There were three bears...three bears;
One was the mama bear, one was the papa bear and one was the wee bear,
The what bear? The wee bear. ch-ch-ch-ch-ch ch-ch-ch-ch.

One day they went a-walkin' in the wee woods a-talkin',
Along came a little girl with long golden curly curls
And her name was Goldilocks,
And up upon the door she knocked.

No one was there, no one was there,
So she walked right in and had herself a ball
Just a-rockin' and a-eatin' and a-sleepin' and all.
ch-ch-ch-ch-ch-ch-ch-ch-ch.

Then home, home, came the three bears,
I said the three, I said the three, I said the three bears
ch-ch-ch-ch-ch-ch-ch-ch-ch

"Who's been eatin' my porridge?" said the papa bear, said the papa bear.
"Who's been eatin' my porridge?" said the mama bear, said the mama bear.
"Bee-bob-a-ree-bear," said the little wee bear, "my porridge is gone!"
(*clap*) (*blow*) AHH!
ch-ch-ch-ch-ch-ch-ch-ch-ch

"Who's been sittin' in my chair?" said the papa bear, said the papa bear.
"Who's been sittin' in my chair?" said the mama bear, said the mama bear.
"Bee-bob-a-ree-bear," said the little wee bear, "my chair is broke."
(*clap*) (*blow*) AHH!
ch-ch-ch-ch-ch-ch-ch-ch-ch

"Who's been sleepin' in my bed?" said the papa bear, said the papa bear.
"Who's been sleepin' in my bed?" said the mama bear, said the mama bear.
"Bee-bob-a-ree-bear," said the little wee bear, "Someone's in my bed!"
(*clap*) (*blow*) AHH!
ch-ch-ch-ch-ch-ch-ch-ch-ch

Then Goldilocks woke up and broke up the party and beat it out of there.
"Bye,bye-bye, bye," said the papa bear, said the papa bear,
"Bye,bye-bye, bye," said the mama bear, said the mama bear,
"Bee-bob-a-ree-bear," said the little wee bear,
And that is the story of the three bears,
I said the three, I said the three, I said the three bears!

Since this song is so long, teach it by sections over a few days.
Having the children echo your recitation works best.

109

LARGE GROUP TIME

CLAP THE BEAT. Children can clap to the beat or use rhythm sticks while reciting this chant. Don't forget, children usually can not keep a beat until they are around five or six years old.

MAKE UP MOTIONS. The children look really cute wagging their fingers and using a low voice for the papa bear. They can put their hands on their wiggling hips and use a medium voice for the mama bear. For the baby bear, they can use the pointer finger on each hand and alternate each pointing up high on, "Bee-bob-a-ree-bear."

PLAY INSTRUMENTS. Each bear could be represented by a different instrument. When that bear talks, the children assigned that instrument part can play.

CURRICULUM INTEGRATION

GOLDILOCK AND THE THREE BEARS
BEARS
FAMILIES

SCIENCE

COOK "PORRIDGE." Oatmeal is the closest food to porridge. Cook some oatmeal following the directions on the package. Serve it for snacktime along with a selection of toppings such as milk, raisins, nuts, and granola.

WARM OR COLD WATER. Provide three tubs or bowls of water that are different temperatures. One could be warm (not hot!), one tepid and one cold. Let the children explore the different temperatures with their hands and spoons.

HARD AND SOFT. Give the children a variety of hard and soft items to sort in the appropriate category.

MATH

GO TOGETHERS. Put out sets of kitchen items that go together in small, medium and large sizes. For example bowls and spoons, cups and straws, salt and pepper. The children can match things that go together and put the correct sizes together.

110

GROUPS OF THREE. Ask the children to bring three items from in the room to Circle Time. Have them talk about what they brought. Count how many items there are all together.

MATCHING BEARS. Cut out bear shapes in small, medium and large sizes. Give each child a bear that will match one of the bear sizes. Place the small, medium and large cut outs where all the children can see. They can match their bear to the cut out. To make it more complicated, they can also match a pattern or facial features drawn on the bears.

TEDDY BEAR COUNTERS. Purchase teddy bear counters from an educational supply catalog. The children can sort and classify, color match or practice addition and subtraction with the bears.

ART

MASKS OR PUPPETS. Children can construct Goldilocks and three bears masks or puppets using paper plates. For masks, cut out circles for eyes and attach yarn or elastic thread to secure the mask around a child's head. For puppets, tape a popsicle stick or tongue depressor to the bottom edge of the plate. Add features with yarn, construction paper, markers and crayons, fabric, etc.

TEXTURE BOOK OR MURAL. Label sections on a large piece of butcher paper or label pages for a book "hard/ soft/ just right." Provide a choice of collage materials that the children can look through and glue in the appropriate section.

BEAR HEADBANDS. Children can make "bear ears" headbands in small, medium and large sizes for the appropriate bear in the story.

WHOLE LANGUAGE / READING

SAME STORY, DIFFERENT STORY. There are numerous versions of Goldilocks and the Three Bears. Read different versions of the story and compare and contrast them. Which version do the children like best?

WRITE A SEQUEL. Have you ever wondered where Goldilocks went or what she did after running from the three bears? How about the three bears. Did they call the police or chase after Goldilocks? Ask the children what happened next and write a sequel.

MULTI-CULTURAL

BEARS AROUND THE WORLD. Bears live in many countries around the world. Go to the library and get books on bears such as the Asian black bear, the sun bear from China, the sloth bear from Indochina, and the spectacled bear from the Andes.

RELATED ACTIVITIES

THE THREE BEARS' HOUSE. Set up this storybook house by placing three chairs, bowls and spoons, and three beds (use blankets, cushions or mattresses) of small medium and large size in the housekeeping area. You can have a dress-up box with fuzzy hoods for the bears and a wig for Goldilocks. To encourage boys to be "Goldilocks" change the name to "Goldiboy" and provide a hat for him to wear.

RELATED MUSIC

The Bear Went Over the Mountain
Teddy Bear, Teddy Bear Turn Around
The Bear Hunt (chant)

RELATED LITERATURE

Turkle, Brinton. (1986). **DEEP IN THE FOREST.** New York: Dutton.

BOOKS ABOUT THREE'S:
Appleby, Ellen.(1984). **THREE BILLY GOAT'S GRUFF: A NORWEGIAN FOLKTALE.** New York: Scholastic.

Galdone, Paul.(1981). **THE THREE BEARS.** New York: Putnam.

Galdone, Paul. (1970). **THREE LITTLE PIGS.** New York: Clarion.

Ivimey, John. (1970). **THREE BLIND MICE.** New York: Clarion.

UNO, DOS, TRES, AMIGOS

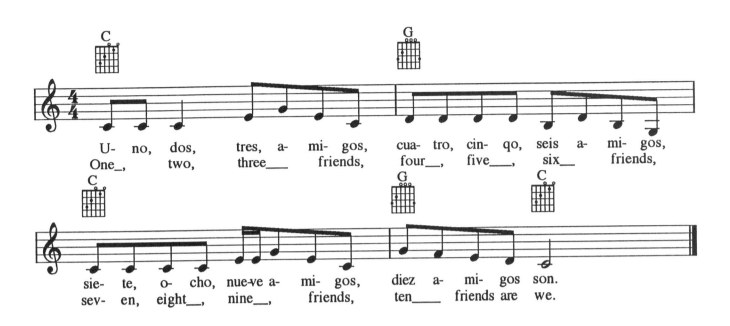

U- no, dos, tres, a- mi- gos, cua- tro, cin- qo, seis a- mi- gos,
One_, two, three___ friends, four__, five___, six__ friends,

sie- te, o- cho, nue-ve a- mi- gos, diez a- mi- gos son.
sev- en, eight__, nine__, friends, ten____ friends are we.

(LARGE GROUP TIME)

COUNTING. Have the children hold up fingers corresponding to the numbers sung.

AMIGO MEANS FRIEND. Have a child stand up for each number sung. On the last number, *diez,* have all the children hold hands.

AMERICAN SIGN LANGUAGE. Teach the children to sign the numbers and/or words in American Sign Language. Consult a dictionary on ASL or contact a local Center on Deafness.

NUMBER CARDS. Give each of the children a card with a number one through ten written on it. When you sing that number, the child with that number card stands up and shows their card.

(CURRICULUM INTEGRATION)

COUNTING
FRIENDS
MEXICO
SPAIN

COOK A MEXICAN TREAT. Tortillas, guacamole, tacos, and flan are just a few Mexican specialties that are easy to prepare and delicious to eat. Here's a recipe for flour tortillas:

2 cups flour
1 tsp. salt
1/4 cup shortening
1/2 cup lukewarm water

Put all ingredients in a medium size bowl and mix thoroughly. Knead with hands until it makes a stiff dough. If too dry add more water, if too wet, add more flour. If you refrigerate the dough for 24 hours, it may be easier to handle. Roll into balls that you will flatten into 7 inch rounds. An adult drops each tortilla onto a very hot ungreased griddle. Bake until it starts to brown on one side. Turn with a spatula to the other side and cook. Serve warm with cheese or butter or cold with butter and honey.

CALLING ALL FRIENDS. Punch a small hole in the bottom of an empty tin can or a plastic cup. Insert a string through the hole in one cup from the inside to the outside. Tie the string on the inside around a toothpick or small nail so that the string doesn't come out. Do the same with the other cup. One child puts the cup over his/her ear. Another child pulls the string taut and talks into the other cup. The sound should travel down the string into the cup where the sound is amplified. The string must be pulled taut and have no one touching it in order for this to work.

FLANNELBOARD COUNTING. Have the children put feltboard numbers or figures of children on the flannelboard while you sing the song. You could even glue felt onto the back of photographs of children in your class and put them up on the flannelboard while you sing.

FOOD COUNTING. Give each child a bag containing ten raisins or pretzels. Sing, "One little, two little, three little pretzels (or raisins.") As you sing, the children count the items in their bag. You can then sing the song backwards starting with ten and ending with one.

GROUPS OF TEN. Ask the children to bring ten of one item to school. Explore, compare and discuss the items they brought in. For children over four years old, count by tens to find out how many items there are all together. Combine the objects and have the children sort them into similar groups.

ART

FRIENDSHIP NECKLACES. Give each child a piece of yarn or thread, some "o" shaped cereal, and cut pieces of straws. They can make a necklace which, when completed, they will give to a friend.

FRIENDSHIP PAINTING. Each child chooses a friend with whom he or she will paint on a large paper or the easel.

FRIENDSHIP COLLAGE. Two children work together cutting out magazine pictures and gluing them onto a sheet of paper.

PINATA. You can make a pinata with your class by having children paper mache over a blown up balloon. When dry, paint it or decorate with crepe paper. Cut a small flap in the bottom, fill with prizes and tape the flap closed. Hang the pinata from the ceiling and have children take turns trying to knock down the pinata with a broomstick while blindfolded or with their eyes closed.

WHOLE LANGUAGE / READING

'UNO, DOS, TRES AMIGOS" BOOK. Write the numerals on each page and use photographs of the children on each page to illustrate the number represented. Count high enough to get each child's photo into the book.

COUNT OTHER THINGS THAN "AMIGOS." Learn other words of things to count in Spanish. Write the Spanish word and the English word along with a picture of the item and sing the song. For example:
    shoes-*zapatos*
    heads- *cabezas*

MULTI-CULTURAL

COUNT IN OTHER LANGUAGES. It is easy to translate this song into other languages. Ask parents in your class who may speak another language to help. You could also get the information from the language department of a local university or college.

EXPLORE ANOTHER CULTURE. Ask parents in your class to come in and share part of their heritage with your class. They could present a tradition, food, ethnic costume, story or talk about what it was like to grow up in their particular cultural environment.

RELATED ACTIVITIES

MEXICAN FIESTA. Invite families to a Mexican fiesta. Cinco de Mayo (May 5) is a great holiday to celebrate together. Serve Mexican food the children have prepared along with treats sent by parents. The children can perform "Uno, Dos, Tres Amigos" and any other Mexican songs or dances they've learned (the Mexican Hat Dance "La Raspa" is an easy one.)

RELATED MUSIC

La Raspa
De Colores
The More We Get Together
Ten in the Bed

RELATED LITERATURE

Behrens, Jane. (1982). **FIESTA!: CINCO DE MAYO.** Chicago: Children's Press.

Hill, Eric. (1989). **LA HERMANITA DE SPOT.** New York: G.P. Putnam and Sons.

(1991).**MY FIRST 100 WORDS IN SPANISH AND ENGLISH.** New York: Simon and Schuster.

WHAT ARE YOU WEARING

Words and Music by   Hap Palmer

*Continue singing verses about different clothing items i.e. shoes, socks,
long sleeves, short sleeves, tights, hair ribbons, buttons, zippers, etc.*

117

SING IT AGAIN. This is a wonderful opening song for starting the day. Look around the room and sing about the various colors, designs and types of clothing that the children are wearing. If children are very young, have special needs or if you're introducing a new concept such as polka dots or plaid, tell them what to look for in their clothing before you sing the verse so that they have time to mentally process it before they stand up.

CLAP HANDS, HOP AROUND. Change "stand up" to "clap hands" or "hop around." The children can give you ideas for what activity to do.

WHAT ARE YOU PLAYING? Instead of "what are you wearing," give the children instruments and sing, "What are you playing?"
>   If you're playing the bells, stand up...

SING ABOUT DRESSING UP. Use this song for Storybook Dress-up Day, Halloween and for community helpers week. The children wear a costume and we sing about what they are dressed up as:
>   If you're dressed as Cinderella, stand up...
>   If you're dressed as a doctor, stand up...

HOW ARE YOU FEELING? Sing about how the children are feeling by changing the words:
>   How are you feeling, how are you feeling...
>   If you're feeling happy (sad, silly, angry) stand up...

FOR PLANNING OR CHOICE TIME. In order for the children to choose in which area they will play, you can sing:
>   Where are you going (working, playing), where are you going...
>   If you're going to paint, stand up...

FIVE SENSES. Give each of the children something different to eat, touch, smell or look at. Sing about the five senses by changing the words:
>   What are you seeing (touching, smelling, tasting, etc)...
>   If you see the color red, (touching something yellow)...

CURRICULUM INTEGRATION

CLOTHING
COLORS
EMOTIONS
FIVE SENSES
COMMUNITY HELPERS

SCIENCE

FASTENERS DISPLAY. On your science table display all sort of fasteners used for clothing such as buttons, hooks and eyes, zippers, buckles, snaps, velcro, clips, laces, clips, etc.

FEELY BOX OR SACK. Put four different items of clothing in a box or sack (a pillow case works well) into which the children cannot see. Ask one child to reach in and either describe the texture(s) and shape to the other children or to tell everyone what he/she feels. You can use doll clothing so that the items are small enough to go into a bag. You can also place items with different textures or shapes in the feely sack. Ask a child to pull out the item that is soft (rough, smooth, hard, bumpy, sticky) or the item that is round (square, flat, triangular.) For older children give the item that is to be found two attributes (for example, round *and* bumpy.)

WHAT TO WEAR? Bring in a sack of clothing some of which you only wear in cold weather and some of which you only wear in warm weather. Tell the children that you are going on a vacation where it will be very, very cold. Hold up each article of clothing and have them tell you if it is appropriate to wear in cold weather. You can do the same activity but describe a warm place to which you will be going.

MITTENS AND ICE CUBES. Give each child a mitten that he/she is to place on one hand. Then pass out an ice cube to each child. Have the children hold the ice cube in the hand wearing the mitten and count to 10 or twenty. How did it feel? Now put the ice cube in the hand without the mitten. Count to 10 or twenty while holding the ice cube (if it starts to hurt, put it down.) How did that feel? What happened to the ice cube? Why did it melt when it was in your hand but not when in the mitten? Why is it a good idea to wear mittens and cover your body up when it is cold outside?

MATH

HOW MANY SOCKS? Count how many children in the room are wearing socks? Count how many socks there are. Why are there more socks than there are children? Talk about socks coming in pairs. What else comes in pairs?

SHOE GRAPH. On a large floor graph, place several different types of shoes such as velcros, buckle, hiking, party, boots, and sandals at the top of the grid. All the children look at the type of shoe they are wearing and place their own shoe (which they have removed) under a similar shoe on the graph. Which had the most, the least, the same?

SHORT OR LONG SLEEVES? Make a large cut out of a shirt with a long sleeve on one side and a short sleeve on the other side. Give each child a sticker or sticky dot which the children place on the sleeve of the shirt cut-out depending on which type of shirt they are wearing. How many children are wearing short sleeved shirts? How many are wearing short sleeves?

SHOE MATCHING. Have each child take off one shoe and put it into a shoe pile in the middle of the floor. Ask them to take off the other shoe and put it in a box which you are passing around. When they have removed both shoes, give each child one shoe from the box, making sure that it is not their own shoe. Each child then goes through the pile of shoes on the floor to find the mate to the shoe they are holding. After each child has a matched pair, see if they can remember to which child the pair belongs.

(ART)

CLOTHING PICTURES. Children look through magazines and cut and glue pictures of specific items of clothing. You can have them search for shirts, hats, socks, winter clothes, summer clothes, red clothing, polka dots, stripes, etc.

PUT ON A HAPPY FACE. Provide the children with a sheet of paper on which you have drawn a large circle. Describe that this is a face but you don't know if she's wearing a happy, say, angry , sleepy, or silly face. Each child decides what type of face their person will wear and draws it with a marker or crayon. Have them tell you why he/she is feeling that way.

TEXTURE OR FABRIC COLLAGE. Children can make collages of materials with different textures or with fabric swatches with different patterns and textures. You could prepare large paper doll shape cut-outs on which they glue the collage materials for clothing.

(WHOLE LANGUAGE / READING)

ANIMALS SHOULD DEFINITELY NOT WEAR CLOTHING. Read this fun book by Judi Barrett with children. Have the class come up with a list of other animals you could include in their version of this book. Come up with funny ideas of the clothing items those animals should not wear and why.   You also could put a new twist on this idea and write a book "Animals Definately *Should* Wear Clothing."You could ask some children from an older classroom to help illustrate the new version.

120

WORD CHART. As a heading on a chart, write parts of the body or show pictures of parts of the body such as head, neck, torso, arms, legs, feet, hands. Go through the different parts and have the children tell you what types of clothing we wear on each part of the body. Write the word under each heading.

MULTI-CULTURAL

CHILDREN AT HOME AND AROUND THE WORLD. Look at pictures of children from different ethnic backgrounds. Are they dressed the same or differently than the children in your classroom? By showing pictures of children from ethnically diverse backgrounds, the children can see how children in their own country dress the same regardless of the color of their skin, but if they live in another country, they may dress differently.

RELATED ACTIVITIES

COMMUNITY HELPERS. Many community helpers can be identified by the clothing they wear that is specific to their job. Which jobs can the children think of that require special clothing or uniforms? Show pictures of community helpers and have the children tell you what their job is. Educational supply catalogs often have community helper posters or cards you can purchase.

TOUCHING TEXTURES. Have children look carefully at their clothing and touch something smooth, soft, hard, or bumpy. They can also touch clothing that is a specific color, design or worn on a specific part of their body.

SPECIAL CLOTHING DAY. Once a week or once a month, ask the children all wear a specific clothing item such as a hat, or the color yellow, or funny socks, mismatched shoes, etc.

RELATED MUSIC

Mary's Wearing A Red Dress
Miss Mary Mack

RELATED LITERATURE

Barrett, Judi. (1970). Illustrated by Ron Barrett. **ANIMALS SHOULD DEFINITELY NOT WEAR CLOTHING.** New York: Atheneum.

Carlstrom, Nancy White. (1986). Illustrated by Bruce Degen. **JESSE BEAR, WHAT WILL YOU WEAR?** New York: MacMillan Publishing.

Peek, Merle. (1985). **MARY WORE HER RED DRESS AND HENRY WORE HIS GREEN SNEAKERS.** New York: Clarion Books.

Slobodinka, Bruce. (1991). **CAPS FOR SALE.** New York: W.R. Scott.

REPRODUCIBLE

MINI- BOOKS

(Copy one mini- book per child. Fold each page in half horizontally
and then again in half vertically)

1.   2.   3.

Apples and Bananas

Draw something you like to eat.

I like to eat, eat, eat apples and bananas.

I like to ate, ate, ate aypuls and banaynays.

I like to eet, eet, eet, eeples and baneenees.

I like to ite, ite, ite, iples and baninis.

I like to ote, ote, ote, oples and banonos.

I like to ute, ute, ute, uples and banunus.

Baby Bird

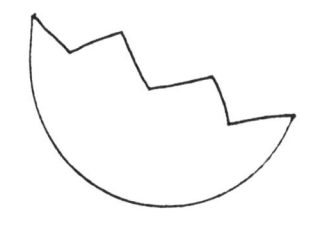

Draw what you think has hatched from the egg.

Here's a baby bird,
He's hatching from his
   shell,
Out pops his head,
And then comes his tail.
Now his legs he
   stretches,
His wings he gives a flap,
And then he flies and
   flies and flies,
Now what do you think
   of that?
Down, down, down,
Down down, down,
Down, down... BOOM!

Did You Feed My Cow?

Draw your favorite farm animal.

Did you feed my cow?   (Yes, Ma'am)
Did you feed my cow?   (Yes, Ma'am)
Well, what did you feed her?   (Corn and hay)
Well, what did you feed her?   (Corn and hay)

Did you milk her good?   (Yes, Ma'am)
Did you milk her like you should? (Yes, Ma'am)
Well, how did you milk her? (Squish, squish, squish)
Well, how did you milk her? (Squish, squish, squish)

Did my cow get sick?   (Yes, Ma'am)
Was she covered with tick?   (Yes, Ma'am)
Well, how did she die?   (M-m-m-m)
Well, how did she die?   (M-m-m-m)

Did the buzzards come?   (Yes, Ma'am)
Did the buzzards come?   (Yes, Ma'am)
Well, how did they come? (Flop, flop, flop)
Well, how did they come? (Flop, flop, flop)
How did they come?   (Flop, flop, flop)
And that was the end of the cow.

Dreidl Song

I have a little dreidl,
I made it out of clay,
And when it's dry and ready,
Then dreidl I shall play.

Oh, dreidl, dreidl, dreidl,
I made it out of clay,
Oh, dreidl, dreidl, dreidl,
Now dreidl I shall play.

It has a lovely body,
With legs so short and thin,
And when it gets all tired,
It drops and then I win.

Oh, dreidl, dreidl, dreidl,
I made it out of clay,
Oh, dreidl, dreidl, dreidl,
Now dreidl I shall play.

If you had a lump of clay, what would you make? Draw a picture of it.

Five Little Pumpkins

Draw your favorite jack-o-lantern
 face.

Five little pumpkins sitting on a gate,
The first one said, "Oh, my it's getting
        late!"
The second one said, "There are
        witches in the air!"
The third one said, "We don't care!"
The fourth one said, "Let's run and run
and run;"
The fifth one said, "I'm ready for some
        fun!"
"Oo-oo," went the wind and out went
        the light,
And the five little pumpkins rolled out
        of sight.

Hush Little Baby

What would you want your mother or father to buy for you? Draw a picture of it.

Hush little baby, don't say a word,
Papa's going to buy you a mockingbird.
If that mockingbird don't sing,
Papa's gonna buy you a diamond ring.
If that diamond ring turns brass,
Papa's gonna buy you a looking glass.
If that looking glass gets broke,
Papa's gonna buy you a billy goat.
If that billy goat don't pull,
Papa's gonna buy you a cart and bull.
If that cart and bull turn over,
Papa's gonna buy you a dog named Rover.
If that dog named Rover don't bark,
Papa's gonnà buy you a horse and cart.
If that horse and cart fall down,
You'll still be the sweetest little baby in town.

I'm Me,
I'm Special

You are special. Draw a picture of yourself.

I'm me and I'm special,
There's no one else that's just like me.
I'm me and I'm special,
Take a look and you can see.
I'm about this tall and I've got this skin,
Just the right size for me to grow up in,
I'm me and I'm special,
There's no one else that's just like me.
I'm me and I'm special,
There's no one else that's just like me.
I'm me and I'm special,
Take a look and you can see.
I've got a great big smile and I love to laugh,
I don't even mind it when I take a bath.
I'm me and I'm special,
There's no one else that's just like me.

Jingle Bells

What do you like best about winter? Draw a winter picture.

Dashing through the snow in a
one horse open sleigh,
O'er the fields we go
Laughing all the way.
Bells on bobtail ring,
Making spirits bright,
What fun it is to ride and sing
A sleighing song tonight.

Jingle bells, jingle bells,
Jingle all the way.
Oh, what fun it is to ride in a one
horse open sleigh, Hey!
Jingle bells, jingle bells,
Jingle all the way.
Oh, what fun it is to ride in a one
horse open sleigh.

Miss Lucy
Had A Baby

Draw a picture of what you
looked like as a baby.

Miss Lucy had a baby,
She named him Tiny Tim,
She put him in the bathtub
To see if he could swim.

He drank up all the water,
He ate up all the soap,
He tried to eat the bathtub,
But it wouldn't go down his throat.

Miss Lucy called the doctor,
Miss Lucy called the nurse,
Miss Lucy called the lady
With the alligator purse.

Miss Mary Mack

How high can you jump? Draw yourself jumping and touching something very high.

Miss Mary Mack, Mack, Mack,
All dressed in black, black, black,
With silver buttons, buttons,
    buttons,
Up and down her back, back,
    back.

She asked her mother, mother,
    mother,
For fifteen cents, cents, cents,
To watch the elephants, elephants,
    elephants,
Jump the fence, fence, fence.

They jumped so high, high, high,
They reached the sky, sky, sky,
And they didn't come back, back,
    back,
'Til the fourth of July, ly, ly.

The Mulberry
Bush

Draw a picture of something you
do early in the morning.

Here we go 'round the mulberry bush,
The mulberry bush, the mulberry bush.
Here we go 'round the mulberry bush
So early in the morning.

This is the way we wash our face,
Wash our face, wash our face.
This is the way we wash our face
So early in the morning.

This is the way we comb our hair,
Comb our hair, comb our hair.
This is the way we comb our hair
So early in the morning.

This is the way we brush our teeth,
Brush our teeth, brush our teeth.
This is the way we brush our teeth
So early in the morning.

My Aunt Came Back

What would you like your aunt to bring you from her vacation? Draw a picture of it.

My aunt came back from
    Timbuctu,
She brought with her
A wooden shoe.

My aunt came back from
    old Algiers,
She brought with her
A pair of shears.

My aunt came back from
    old Japan,
She brought with her
A paper fan.

My aunt came back from
    old Belgium,
She brought with her
Some bubblegum.

My aunt came back from
    the county fair,
She brought with her
A rocking chair.

Oh, When the Saints

Draw your favorite part of a parade.

Oh, when the saints go marching in,

Oh, when the saints go marching in,

Oh, yes, I want to be in that number,

When the saints go marching in.

One Elephant

Draw your favorite friend that you like to play with.

One elephant went out to play
On a spider's web one day,
She had such enormous fun,
She asked for another elephant
    to come.

Two elephants went out to play
On a spider's web one day,
They had such enormous fun,
They asked for another elephant
    to come.

Three elephants went out to play
On a spider's web one day,
They had such enormous fun,
They asked for another elephant
    to come.

Over in the Meadow

Draw your favorite animal.

Over in the meadow in the sand in
the sun,
Lived an old mother turtle and her
little turtle one.
"Dig," said the mother,
"We dig," said the one,
So they dug all day in the sand and
the sun.

Over in the meadow where the
stream runs blue,
Lived an old mother fish and her little
fishes two.
"Swim," said the mother,
"We swim," said the two,
So they swam all day where the
stream ran blue.

Over the
River

Draw a Thanksgiving picture.

Over the river and through the woods,

To grandmother's house we go.

The horse knows the way

To carry the sleigh through the

White and drifted snow.

Over the river and through the woods,

Oh, how the wind does blow,

It stings the nose and bites the toes,

As over the ground we go.

Peanut Butter

Do you like peanut butter and jelly?
Draw how you feel if someone gives you
a peanut butter and jelly sandwich.

Peanut, peanut butter...jelly!
Peanut, peanut butter...jelly!

First you take the peanuts and you
Dig 'em, you dig 'em, you dig'em
Dig 'em, dig 'em;
Then you crush 'em, you crush 'em,
You crush'em, crush 'em, crush 'em;
Then you spread 'em, you spread 'em,
You spread 'em, spread 'em,
Spread 'em.

Then you take the berries and you pick
em, You pick'em, you pick 'em,
Pick 'em, pick 'em;
Then you crush 'em, you crush 'em,
You crush'em, crush 'em, crush 'em;
Then you spread 'em, you spread 'em,
You Spread 'em, spread 'em, spread 'em.

Then you take the sandwich and you
Bite it, you bite it, you bite it, bite it, bite it;
Then you munch it, you munch it,
You munch it, munch it, munch it;
Then you swallow it, you swallow it,
You swallow, swallow, swallow it.

Rain Songs

Draw a picture of a rainy day.

Rain, rain, go away,
Come again another day,
Little Johnny wants to play,
Rain, rain go away.

It's raining, it's pouring,
The old man is snoring,
He went to bed
And he bumped his head ,
And he couldn't get up in the
    morning.

Skinnamarink

Draw a picture of someone you love.

Skinnamarink a dink a dink,
Skinnamarink a doo,
I love you.

Skinnamarink a dink a dink,
Skinnamarink a doo,
I love you.

I love you in the morning and in
the afternoon.
I love you in the evening and
underneath the moon.

Oh,Skinnamarink a dink a dink,
Skinnamarink a doo,
I love you.

Ten in the Bed

Draw your bed? How many people are in it?

There were ten in the bed
And the little one said,
"Roll over, roll over."
So they all rolled over and one
    fell out,
There were nine in the bed
And the little one said,
"Roll over, roll over."
So they all rolled over and one
    fell out,
There were eight in the bed
And the little one said,
"Roll over, roll over."
So they all rolled over and one
    fell out,
There were seven in the bed
And the little one said,
"Roll over, roll over."
So they all rolled over and one
    fell out.

The Ants Go Marching

The ants go marching one by one,
Hurrah, hurrah!
The ants go marching one by one,
Hurrah, hurrah!
The ants go marching one by one,
The little one stops to chew some
    gum,
And they all go marching
Down to the ground, to get out of
    the rain,
Boom, boom, boom!

The ants go marching two by two,
Hurrah, hurrah!
The ants go marching two by two,
Hurrah, hurrah!
The ants go marching two by two,
The little one stops to tie his shoe,
And they all go marching
Down to the ground, to get out of
    the rain,

Draw the little ant stopping to
do something funny.

There's a hole in the bucket,
Dear Liza, dear Liza;
There's a hole in the bucket,
Dear Liza a hole.

Well, fix it, dear Henry,
Dear Henry, dear Henry;
Well, fix it dear Henry,
Dear Henry, fix it.

With what shall I fix it,
Dear Liza, dear Liza?
With what shall I fix it,
Dear Liza, with what?

With a straw, dear Henry,
Dear Henry, dear Henry,
With a straw, dear Henry,
Dear Henry with a straw.

Draw around this hole and make
it into something.

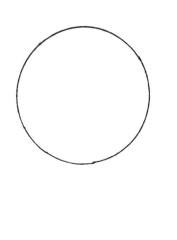

There's a Hole
in the Bucket

This Old Man

Draw "this old man."

This old man, he played one,
He played knick-knack on my thumb.
With a knick-knack paddy-whack
Give the dog a bone,
This old man came rolling home.

This old man, he played two,
He played knick-knack on my shoe.
With a knick-knack paddy-whack
Give the dog a bone,
This old man came rolling home.

This old man, he played three,
He played knick-knack on my knee.
With a knick-knack paddy-whack
Give the dog a bone,
This old man came rolling home.

This old man, he played four,
He played knick-knack on my door.
With a knick-knack paddy-whack
Give the dog a bone,
This old man came rolling home.

Three Bears Chant

Draw your favorite part of
"Goldilocks and the Three Bears."

Once upon a time in a nursery rhyme
There were three bears, three bears;
One was the mama bear,
One was the papa bear,
And one was the wee bear,
The what bear?
The wee bear.
Ch-ch-ch-ch-ch-ch-ch-ch-ch

One day they went a-walkin'
In the wee woods a talkin',
Along came a little girl
With long, golden curly curls,
And her name was Goldilocks.
And up upon the door she knocked.

No one was there,
No one was there,
So she walked right in
And had herself a ball,
Just a-rockin' and a-eatin'
And a-sleepin' and all.
Ch-ch-ch-ch-ch-ch-ch-ch-ch

One, two, three friends,
Four, five, six friends,
Seven, eight, nine friends,
Ten friends are we.

Uno, dos, tres amigos,
Cuatro, cinco, seis amigos,
Siete, ocho, nueve amigos,
Diez amigos son.

Draw a picture of your friends.

Uno, Dos, Tres Amigos

What Are You
Wearing?

What are you wearing today?
Draw a picture of yourself.

What are you wearing?
What are you wearing?
What are you wearing today,
   today?

What are you wearing?
What are you wearing?
What are you wearing today,
   today?

If you're wearing a shirt, stand up,
If you're wearing a shirt, stand up.

If you're wearing a dress, stand up.
If you're wearing a dress, stand up.

If you're wearing red, stand up.
If you're wearing red, stand up.

CIRCLE TIME- Also known as *Large Group Time, Group Time.* This is the time of day when all the children are taught as one large group as opposed breaking into small groups. In preschool and in kindergarten the children are often seated in a circle on the floor.

COLLAGE- An assortment of materials arranged and glued on a paper or another background.

FELTBOARD- Also known as a *flannelboard.* A board covered with flannel or felt on which you can stick pictures made of flannel or felt or pictures with flannel or felt backings. These can be purchased at educational supply stores or through their catalogs or you can easily make one by gluing or stapling flannel or felt to a heavy backing.

FLANNELBOARD- See *feltboard.*

GRAPH- A grid on which items, stickers, or dots can be placed to reinforce the concepts of more, less, or the same. Graphs can be purchased through educational supply catalogs or stores. You can make graphs yourself by drawing a grid on large paper, posterboard, or on a tarp.

INSTRUMENTS- For purposes of this book, *instruments* refers to the variety of percussion and rhythm instruments available for children to use for which they need no formal instruction. They include instruments like, jingle taps, rhythm sticks, sandblocks, tambourines, castanets, triangles. These can be purchased through educational supply catalogs or stores. There are are several good books available through the library that provide instruction for making your own instruments.

NUMBER CARDS- Cards that consist of a numeral and/ or pictures representing the corresponding number.

PITCH- How high or low a sound is.

POCKET CHART- A chart that hangs on the wall or on a chart holder in which their are clear pockets for placing picture or word cards. This can be purchased through educational supply catalogs or stores.

RHYME BANK- A collection of rhyming words kept for the purpose of aiding with writing poems and songs. A rhyme bank can be kept on posters or chart paper, or on index cards. Sets of rhyme cards can be ordered from *Panda Bear Publications, P.O. Box 391, Manitou Springs, Colorado, 80829. See order form at the end of this book.*

SORT AND CLASSIFY- Taking a group of objects and sorting them according to color, shape, texture, use or other attributes.

TEMPO- How fast or slow the beat goes.

WORDCHART- A chart on which you write words related to a particular theme, subject or topic.

INDEX OF THEMES

Following is a list of theme units that work well with particular songs. An * indicates that the words will have to be changed in order for the song to fit the them unit.

ANIMALS
Baby Bird
Did you Feed My Cow
Miss Mary Mack
Over In The Meadow

ALL ABOUT ME
I'm Me, I'm Special

ANTS
The Ants Go Marching

APPLES
Apples and Bananas

AROUND THE WORLD
My Aunt Came Back

BABIES
Baby Bird
Hush Little Baby
Miss Lucy
Over In the Meadow

BEARS
Three Bears Chant

BONES
This Old Man

BUBBLES
Miss Lucy

BUCKETS
There's a Hole... Bucket

CIRCUS
Miss Mary Mack
One Elephant

CLOTHING
What Are You Wearing

COLORS
Miss Mary Mack
What Are You Wearing

COMING TO SCHOOL
Mulberry Bush

COMMUNITY HELPERS
Miss Lucy
There's A Hole... Bucket
What Are You Wearing

COUNTING
The Ants Go Marching
Five Little Pumpkins
Over In the Meadow
Ten In the Bed
This Old Man
Uno, Dos, Tres Amigos

CHRISTMAS
Jingle Bells

DINOSAURS
Baby Bird*
One Elephant*

EGGS
Baby Bird

ELEPHANTS
Miss Mary Mack
One Elephant

EMOTIONS
What Are You Wearing

FAMILIES
Hush Little Baby
Over In The Meadow
Three Bears Chant

FARMS
Did You Feed My Cow
Peanut Butter

FIVE SENSES
Apples and Bananas
Oh, When The Saints

FRIENDS
One Elephant
Skinnamarink
Uno, Dos, Tres Amigos

HABITATS
Over In The Meadow

INDEX OF THEMES

Following is a list of theme units that work well with particular songs. An * indicates that the words will have to be changed in order for the song to fit the them unit.

HALLOWEEN
Five Litle Pumpkins
What Are You Wearing

HANUKKAH
Dreidl Song

HEALTH
Mulberry Bush

HOLES
There's A Hole...Bucket

HYGIENE
Mulberry Bush

INSECTS
The Ants Go Marching
One Elephant

MEXICO
My Aunt Came Back*
Uno, Dos, Tres Amigos

MOTHER'S DAY
Skinnamarink

NATIVE AMERICANS
Over the River

NIGHT / BEDTIME
Ten in the Bed

NUTRITION
Apples and Bananas
Peanut Butter

PATRIOTIC HOLIDAYS
Oh, When the Saints

PETS
This Old Man

PLANTING
Mulberry Bush*

PUMPKINS
Five Little Pumpkins

RAIN
Rain Songs

SAFETY
Mulberry Bush*

SHOES
This Old Man

SPAIN
My Aunt Came Back*
Uno, Dos, Tres Amigos

SPRINGTIME
Mulberry Bush*

SPIDERS
One Elephant

STORYBOOK
What Are You Wearing

THANKSGIVING
Over the River

TRANSPORTATION
My Aunt Came Back

TRAVEL
My Aunt Came Back

VACATION
My Aunt Came Back

VALENTINE'S DAY
Skinnamarink

WATER
Rain Songs

WEATHER
Miss Lucy
Rain Songs

WINTER
Jingle Bells

WINTER HOLIDAYS
Dreidl Song
Jingle Bells

ZOO
One Elephant

Brown, Sam Ed. **BUBBLES, RAINBOWS, & WORMS.** Mt. Rainier, Maryland: Gryphon House.

Burton, Stephanie and Campbell, Phyllis.(1996.) **SCIENCE TIMES WITH NURSERY RHYMES.**Manitou Springs, CO.: Panda Bear Publications.

Burton, Stephanie. (1994). **MUSIC EXPLOSION!!.** Des Moines, Ia.: Perfection Learning Corp.

Coletta, Anthony J. and Kathleen Coletta. (1986). **YEAR 'ROUND ACTIVITIES FOR FOUR YEAR OLD CHILDREN.** West Nyack, N.Y.: Center For Applied Research.

Flemming, Bonnie Mack, and Darlene Softley Hamilton. (1977). **RESOURCES FOR CREATIVE TEACHING IN EARLY CHILDHOOD EDUCATION**. New York: Harcourt Brace Jovanovich.

Raines, Shirley and Robert Canady.(1989). **STORY STRETCHERS.** Mt. Rainier, Maryland: Gryphon House.

Richards, Helen Richards. **THE CHILD IN DEPTH.** California.

Scelsa, Greg and Steve Millang. (1986). **WE ALL LIVE TOGETHER SONG AND ACTIVITY BOOK.** Van Nuys, Ca.: Alfred Publishing Co.

Sobut, Mary A. and Bonnie Neuman Bogen.(1991). **COMPLETE EARLY CHILDHOOD CURRICULUM RESOURCE.** West Nyack, New York: The Center for Applied Research in Education.

Stone, Janet.(1990). **HANDS ON MATH.** Glenview, Illinois: Good Year Books.

Wilmes, Liz and Dick. **EVERYDAY CIRCLE TIMES.** Elgin,Illinois: Building Blocks.

If you borrowed this, why not order one for yourself?
PANDA BEAR PUBLICATIONS...
created by early childhood teachers for early childhood teachers!

MUSIC MANIA book..$19.95
MUSIC MANIA book and cassette..$29.95
MUSIC MANIA book and CD...$33.95
Make the most of your students' brain power with these easy and fun ideas for teaching across the curriculum. *Music Mania* contains 26 favorite children's songs with over 500 activities in reading, science, math, art, circle time and more. Available with or without recordings that provide the songs for each complete learning unit.

MUSIC EXPLOSION book and cassette...$39.95
Recipient of Early Childhood News Award
A complete early childhood curriculum, *Music Explosion* contains 34 classic childhood songs that introduce themes and activities across the curriculum. Includes an audio cassette and a large binder full of great activities for reading, math, science, art, circle time and more.

SCIENCE TIMES WITH NURSERY RHYMES..$16.95
Start with a nursery rhyme, then jump into science! *Science Times with Nursery Rhymes* contains 12 popular nursery rhymes each of which is followed by 5 hands-on science experiences that relate to a concept found in the rhyme. With "Jack and Jill" discover the effects of gravity. "Mary, Mary, Quite Contrary" will lead you to the world of plants. "Roses are Red" encourages exploration of the five senses.

THE CURIOSITY SHOP IDEA BOOK with CD...$21.95
THE CURIOSITY SHOP IDEA BOOK with CASSETTE............................$17.95
Fantastic activities to encourage children to think about and explore the world around them. Complete with units on water, food, plants, dinosaurs, the body, and air all with easy to use ideas and great songs that children and teachers love. Each ideas comes with your choice of CD or cassette.

Title	Qty	Each	Total

SUBTOTAL	
CO res.add 3% sales tax	
Shipping & Handling add 15%	
TOTAL (must be in U.S. funds)	

Call us or mail or fax this form to:
Panda Bear Publications
P.O. Box 391
Manitou Springs, CO 80829
Fax: (719) 685-4427
Phone: (719) 685-3319
www.pandabooks.com
e-mail: burtfam @ netscape.net

I am paying with check, money order, Mastercard, or Visa (circle one):
Credit card #_____
Exp._____
Name on card_____
Signature_____

Name_____
Address_____
City, State, Zip_____
Phone (___) _____

If you borrowed this, why not order one for yourself?
PANDA BEAR PUBLICATIONS...
created by early childhood teachers for early childhood teachers!

MUSIC MANIA book...$19.95
MUSIC MANIA book and cassette...$29.95
MUSIC MANIA book and CD..$33.95
Make the most of your students' brain power with these easy and fun ideas for teaching across the curriculum. *Music Mania* contains 26 favorite children's songs with over 500 activities in reading, science, math, art, circle time and more. Available with or without recordings that provide the songs for each complete learning unit.

MUSIC EXPLOSION book and cassette..$39.95
Recipient of Early Childhood News Award
A complete early childhood curriculum, *Music Explosion* contains 34 classic childhood songs that introduce themes and activities across the curriculum. Includes an audio cassette and a large binder full of great activities for reading, math, science, art, circle time and more.

SCIENCE TIMES WITH NURSERY RHYMES.......................................$16.95
Start with a nursery rhyme, then jump into science! *Science Times with Nursery Rhymes* contains 12 popular nursery rhymes each of which is followed by 5 hands-on science experiences that relate to a concept found in the rhyme. With "Jack and Jill" discover the effects of gravity. "Mary, Mary, Quite Contrary" will lead you to the world of plants. "Roses are Red" encourages exploration of the five senses.

THE CURIOSITY SHOP IDEA BOOK with CD......................................$21.95
THE CURIOSITY SHOP IDEA BOOK with CASSETTE.......................$17.95
Fantastic activities to encourage children to think about and explore the world around them. Complete with units on water, food, plants, dinosaurs, the body, and air all with easy to use ideas and great songs that children and teachers love. Each ideas comes with your choice of CD or cassette.

Title	Qty	Each	Total
	SUBTOTAL		
	CO res.add 3% sales tax		
	Shipping & Handling add 15%		
	TOTAL (must be in U.S. funds)		

Call us or mail or fax this form to:
Panda Bear Publications
P.O. Box 391
Manitou Springs, CO 80829
Fax: (719) 685-4427
Phone: (719) 685-3319
www.pandabooks.com
e-mail: burtfam @ netscape.net

I am paying with check, money order, Mastercard, or Visa (circle one):
Credit card #_____
Exp._____
Name on card_____

Name_____
Address_____
City, State, Zip_____
Phone (___) _____

Signature_____

If you borrowed this, why not order one for yourself?
PANDA BEAR PUBLICATIONS...
created by early childhood teachers for early childhood teachers!

MUSIC MANIA book..$19.95
MUSIC MANIA book and cassette..$29.95
MUSIC MANIA book and CD...$33.95

Make the most of your students' brain power with these easy and fun ideas for teaching across the curriculum. *Music Mania* contains 26 favorite children's songs with over 500 activities in reading, science, math, art, circle time and more. Available with or without recordings that provide the songs for each complete learning unit.

MUSIC EXPLOSION book and cassette..$39.95

Recipient of Early Childhood News Award

A complete early childhood curriculum, *Music Explosion* contains 34 classic childhood songs that introduce themes and activities across the curriculum. Includes an audio cassette and a large binder full of great activities for reading, math, science, art, circle time and more.

SCIENCE TIMES WITH NURSERY RHYMES.....................................$16.95

Start with a nursery rhyme, then jump into science! *Science Times with Nursery Rhymes* contains 12 popular nursery rhymes each of which is followed by 5 hands-on science experiences that relate to a concept found in the rhyme. With "Jack and Jill" discover the effects of gravity. "Mary, Mary, Quite Contrary" will lead you to the world of plants. "Roses are Red" encourages exploration of the five senses.

THE CURIOSITY SHOP IDEA BOOK with CD....................................$21.95
THE CURIOSITY SHOP IDEA BOOK with CASSETTE..........................$17.95

Fantastic activities to encourage children to think about and explore the world around them. Complete with units on water, food, plants, dinosaurs, the body, and air all with easy to use ideas and great songs that children and teachers love. Each ideas comes with your choice of CD or cassette.

Title	Qty	Each	Total

SUBTOTAL	
CO res.add 3% sales tax	
Shipping & Handling add 15%	
TOTAL (must be in U.S. funds)	

Call us or mail or fax this form to:
Panda Bear Publications
P.O. Box 391
Manitou Springs, CO 80829
Fax: (719) 685-4427
Phone: (719) 685-3319
www.pandabooks.com
e-mail: burtfam @ netscape.net

I am paying with check, money order, Mastercard, or Visa (circle one):
Credit card #_____
Exp._____
Name on card_____
Signature_____

Name_____
Address_____
City, State, Zip_____
Phone (____) _____